I0622723

STEPPING STONES

Blended families and
bonus parenting
at its best.

ASHA BIANCA & KRISTINE E. VALK

Bianca Valk Publishing, LLC.

Copyright © 2023 Asha Bianca & Kristine E. Valk.

All rights reserved. No part of this book may be used or reproduced by any means, graphic, electronic, or mechanical, including photocopying, recording, taping or by any information storage retrieval system without the written permission of the author except in the case of brief quotations embodied in critical articles and reviews.

Any people depicted in stock imagery provided by Getty Images are models, and such images are being used for illustrative purposes only. Certain stock imagery © Getty Images.

Scripture quotations taken from The Holy Bible, New International Version® NIV® Copyright © 1973 1978 1984 2011 by Biblica, Inc. TM. Used by permission. All rights reserved worldwide.

ISBN (Paperback): 979-8-9880609-0-1
ISBN (Hardback): 979-8-9880609-1-8
ISBN (eBook): 979-8-9880609-2-5

Library of Congress Control Number: 2022923499

"Blended families are woven together by choice, strengthened by love, tested by everything and each are uniquely ours."
~ U N K N O W N

Dedicated to our blended families, you are and
will forever be our favorite people.
We learn how to be more kind, honoring, safe
and bold every day through you.

CONTENTS

INTRODUCTION

Let's start off by saying that no child dreams of being a stepparent, particularly a stepmom. Most movies portray stepmoms as evil people who have negative agendas and ugly motives. Even saying the word, "stepmom" or "step child" can bring to mind someone who is inferior.

We spent a lot of time thinking about the meaning and purpose of the definition "step." Interestingly enough when you look the word up, you'll see words like, "placing one foot in front of the other", or "to go somewhere," and our favorite "to move to a new position." Why then do we have so many negative connotations with being a "stepparent?" How can we change the narrative? Let's be honest, we have been living within this role, and have theorized that the most common reason for this negative portrayal is due to our inherent fear of something different from what is traditionally the norm.

We are brought up to expect there will be one dad, one mom and two children, a white picket fence, and a dog named Fluffy, the only way to have a family. Anything that strays from this simple view of the world creates skepticism and devaluation. This isn't just true of families that are made up differently, it can be true of anything that is different. It is a bias we can tangibly feel, but in today's world different is the norm. There are more blended families than non-blended families and the time to debunk the myth that a blended family can't flourish is _now_.

We realized nearly immediately upon becoming a stepparent ourselves this was one of the most foreign roles we'd ever signed-up for. The lack of preparation, support, honest materials, true stories and all-around shared experiences is real. When we talk within our circles, those who have experience being in a blended family tend to lean towards all the negatives. Searching for some positive experiences seemed to be a novelty. The shortage of game changing resources became a mission for us to help fill this gap.

You'll notice that we use "step" and "bonus" interchangeably throughout this book, and we recommend choosing whichever title works for you and your family. Create conversation around this and have awareness of how each name may be interpreted by children and parents.

The word "step" traditionally has a meaning of movement and within families, stepping up, in, out, etc. We recognize there is change occurring along the highs and lows of navigating through these new relationships. The word "step" can allow for a separation between individuals that may be intentional or not. Why you may want to use "bonus" is because as new members of the family you may wish to be viewed as an addition. We traditionally view any bonus as something very positive or unexpected. Stepparent and children relations will evolve and so will the definition you choose to use.

There can be a stigma associated with the term step that many in the blended community are trying to change. However, some prefer the lighthearted spirit of bonus that references a delightful surprise of blended families. Other children and parents actually refer to themselves as straight up, "mom" or "dad." There are many reasons for different names. The ages that the children are when you enter their lives can be a big factor, such as how much time you spend with them, what your relationship looks like, and how involved their biological parents are. All of these play a factor, however, whatever works for your situation is the right answer for you and your family.

● ● ●

My son and his best friend Josh were inseparable. Whenever Josh was at our house, he called me "mom" all the time. I enjoyed that these boys were close and that I was a "mom" to both. It's a great feeling when your kids' friends view you in this special role. After a few years, Josh's father and I started dating, and then we got married. Now I was Josh's "stepmom," and the first time he said mom after I married his father, he said, Well, that's kind of weird now ... so he decided to call me by my first name. We all just laughed as we had to acknowledge the new family we were now and smiled as we navigate forward. Now it's been years since this happened, and Josh is again calling me "mom." I am glad we all decided on our roles together and what we were comfortable calling each other.

"The only steps in this house are the stair steps and the only half in this house is the half & half creamer."

~AL HODSON

• • •

When I became a grandmother, I wasn't sure what name my stepdaughter was going to use for me. After all, I was the "step-grandma" and didn't want to take anything away from either bio grandmother. So, when my stepdaughter asked me what I wanted to use as a name, I said whatever they felt like calling me. I wanted them to decide. Honestly, I would have been happy with anything. We went back and forth with many different names and ideas, then my son-in-law came up with my "grandma" name, and it felt perfect! I truly feel special! Now I have an extraordinary unique name for us, and the best part is all our grandchildren will use the same name for me. We came up with the perfect name for me together.

We also reference faith many times throughout these pages, both because we as authors have a strong sense of faith and some of those, we interviewed faith created a foundation for their perspective. Many have leaned on their faith to help them through the challenges of being a blended family. Even if you are not a person of a particular faith referenced, this does not mean this book is not for you. Our exploration, stories, and suggestions from those who have traveled this path to you who maybe just starting, will be helpful to your blended family success.

• • •

Becoming a stepparent has been one of the most difficult roles that I've ever **chosen** in my life. If I didn't have my faith to lean into, I would have been so consumed with the challenges that I would have let them overtake me. Prayer has been my constant and best tool.

This book is for every life that is touched by a blended family. There are separate tips for each role in each section. This is intentional so you can read perspectives of your co-parents, family and friends as it relates to a specific topic. While many of you may have one primary role, it is likely that all of you are supportive players in the lives of a blended family that you know. This book is formed by interviews, surveys and experiences from a large number of blended families. Names and stories are adjusted to safeguard specifics and focus on the learning.

This book's purpose is to help us understand different perspectives and thrive as we navigate the highs and lows as a blended family.

The book's content may not apply to your situation today, but it is likely most experiences may have an application somewhere in your life. You, the reader, can take these insights and decide how they may apply to your situation. There is little black and white with blended families; instead, there are a lot of shades of gray, which makes our roles challenging, but also rewarding.

"Family isn't defined only by last names or by blood; it's defined by commitment and love."
~DAVE WILLIS

GET READY!

If you are ...

A soon to be bonus parent, know the wonderfully rewarding, yet difficult role you are about to take on. Know to move into this new important role with eyes wide open. It's our hope to save you some pain by setting expectations and sharing our lessons learned. Ask a good deal of questions, do your homework and do the self-awareness work to know yourself well enough to ensure you bring your best self to this new role. You are a partner to your new spouse, but you are also a partner to their children and past relationships as you enter in.

An existing bonus parent, be encouraged to keep fighting the good fight if there have been struggles and remain committed to loving all involved. Our hope is that you feel validated, heard and appreciated in new ways through reading this book. That you learn it's never too late to have a happily ever after, restore relationships and move forward as a family.

A parent, know you have great influence in how your children will respond to their new bonus parent. Our hope for you is to see this important role you play in welcoming the new family member. We hope you are encouraged when you see someone else loving your child, that you understand they will not do everything perfectly but if their heart is in the right place, there is more than enough love for everyone. We want to reinforce that you make a tremendous difference by honoring this co-parent, or at a minimum, being civil and respectful to them. Our aspiration for you is that you don't become discouraged when changes arise and that you remain steady and committed to your family.

An extended Family, lean in, love well and welcome this important new family member, trust your son or daughter in their decision and support their family fully. Be fair and kind in everything, if in doubt, ask. Be careful about perceived allegiances to exes. Make every effort to support this new blended family, if you're not sure how to, ask them how to engage and what they need for support from you. If they ask you to do or not do something, listen.

To _all_ involved, there is enough love for every kind of family. Don't create your own narratives around gossip or assumptions. If you're curious and have a strong enough relationship to ask about an element, ask the parents gently at a time that is appropriate. Do not ask the children. Keep conversations between adults as much as possible to prevent children from feeling more in the middle more than they already are.

> *"Families don't have to match. You don't have to look like everyone else to love them."*
> ~LEIGH ANNE TUOHY

WHAT I WISH I KNEW

STEP UP

When we think of families from our childhood, we typically think back to the 1950s and the old mantra of a father, mother, son, and daughter—a.k.a. "normal" or a "perfect" family. Growing up we watched movies like *Cinderella* and *Snow White*; these movies illustrated stepmothers as evil. So it's no wonder why families today, regardless of how they are formed, have some preconceived images of blended families. The term *wicked* is generally applied to a stepparent or references to the "redheaded stepchild" to depict something less than human or evil.

Unless you were watching *The Brady Bunch*, rarely were we provided the positive perspectives of how to blend. As the reality of blended families became more the norm, Hollywood started to get closer with sitcoms like *Modern Family* and movies like *Stepmom or Mrs. Doubtfire*. However, honest conversations, real-world lessons, and resources are just now starting to rise, helping new bonus parents navigate this arena. The importance of the stepparent is immense, and much to the contrary of the way our culture has devalued you or made you the villain, you have a tremendous ability to love well in every situation.

> "A good stepparent can literally turn
> the life of a child around."
>
> ~ UNKNOWN

When we first collaborated about writing this book and began inquiring about actual family experiences, the weight of the thought *"I wish I knew then what I know now,"* was significant. Between the authors and the families we interviewed, we have hundreds of years of experience represented and shared in the following pages. Our hope is that we save many new blended families the pain of having to learn these lessons the hard way.

Blended families are not original families, so they take a different level of intentionality, focus, and learning to help create healthy relationships. You can't help what happened before you arrived on the scene, but you can definitely educate yourself and make a difference every day now that you're in the picture.

*"You can't go back and change the beginning,
but you can start where you are and change the ending."*
~ UNKNOWN

Our goal is to provide families with different perspectives to help you navigate through a variety of challenges in a positive manner to benefit the entire family in everyday situations. We'll dive into different positions, circumstances, and values. Take what you can to allow you to move forward in a positive way to better your family. It won't be perfect, and that is OK! Perfect is boring and a myth anyway!

Self-awareness is the key. How we respond, what actions we take, and most of all how we learn to love and become inclusive, is vital. Learning how to be a blended family is a process; envision stepping-stones and the way that, one by one, they take you to a destination. If you have ever walked on stones, you know they are all aligned to show us the way. However, over time some stones may be harder to see because of the circumstances surrounding the area. In these cases, we must learn when to step up, when to step aside, and when to step down. Sometimes we even need to stand still until we have a clear path forward.

"A stepparent doesn't just marry a spouse; they marry their spouse's entire situation. They have to find a balance between supporting and defending without overstepping visible and invisible boundaries."

~ D R .   L A U R A

This quote really resonated with us because many of the boundaries are invisible, so it can feel a bit like walking through a land mine or being caught unprepared in a tropical storm. While weather is unpredictable, so are blended families, we can learn to adapt to the circumstances around us. Most of all, we need to have an open mind and be willing to accept our own actions as well as the actions of others. We don't have to like everyone and agree with every decision; we simply need to be able to understand and sometimes agree to disagree, respectfully.

Understanding the different perspectives is critical for blended families. If we thought parenting was easy, there wouldn't be thousands upon thousands of books, blogs, or articles written. Who knows which approach is right? We have the same challenge. How do we "blend" a family? Let's take a look at those who are in the trenches and have lived through real setbacks and breakthroughs. Like learning to ride a bike, we fall a few times before we learn to balance. Blended families are more aware of balance. It's a fine line that is walked; thus, we want you to think about stepping-stones while you are on this journey.

TAKING THAT FIRST STEP...

Let's start from the beginning. When we think about becoming a stepparent, let's take out the negative and turn it into a positive. Start by identifying ourselves as part of the family support system, a bonus parent, another person dedicated to the joy of the children.

"Stepparents are not around to replace a biological parent, rather to augment a child's life experience."
~AZRIEL JOHNSON

We may think we know a lot about the dynamics and the way the family is going to be. Summed up in one sentence, we really know very little. Even if we have been experiencing the dynamics of the parents while dating, the reality of living together as a new bonus parent will bring new terrain.

Generally, when starting a new relationship, your partner is not going to paint their ex in the best light. It's important to remember there was a day when they believed this person would be their forever. Their children resulted from this belief and love. It is true, in most families, they never thought there would be a divorce. There were things about their partner they loved, and of course things they didn't. These behaviors will likely surface not only in their exes but also potentially through their children. To villainize any person is to ignore the fact that every single person has good and bad traits. Your partner's ex is no different. They also likely had a pattern for co parenting as individuals, particularly if the divorce was some time ago or the marriage was short. There is a rhythm to co-parenting that existed before you were part of the picture and one that you'll want to understand as you learn how to navigate and support your new family.

"Don't worry if you're not an instant happily-ever after family. Expect to endure "I give up" days and rejoice in the "I can do this" days. It will take work, dedication, an excellent sense of humor, and strong resolve. But hey, since when has any family taken the easy route? Don't do "easy"—do "worth it!"

~JESSICA JAMES

The following questions are designed to help before you walk down the aisle and step up as a bonus parent; however, they can help at any time during your journey and provide understanding and perspective. We'll dive deeper into these questions throughout our journey, but these are a good place to start thinking through your responses, before you say, "I do."

STEP UP

- Does documentation exist resolving the big issues with coparenting? What is the documented parenting time, holiday plan, maintenance, and child support that has been court ordered?
- What are the non-negotiables with parenting, and what are the differences that occur at each home?
- What role are the mom and dad hoping you bring as a bonus parent?
- What will my relationship with my stepchildren look like?
- How do we support fairness in blended families?
- What are the plans for when conflict arises?
- Are there any secrets or important information that are not out in the open (e.g., adoptions, self-harm, addictions, previous marriages, other children, infidelity)?

- What if the co-parent is not cooperative?
- What is going to be my go-to when things get really challenging?
- Am I ready for all that comes with being a bonus parent? What are my expectations? Is it worth it? Am I ready to give my all for another's child?
- How will his/hers, mine, and ours come together and feel like they are part of this new family?

Please use this space to journal your thoughts or responses:

_____

_____

_____

_____

_____

_____

_____

_____

_____

_____

"For those of you that say, 'This is not what I signed up for,' remember that life is not built for your comfort. Life is built by lessons that test you, and push you with every possibility of either demolishing your foundation or reinforcing it!"

~ JESSICA JAMES

ADVICE FROM THOSE WHO HAVE WALKED THE PATH

• • •

Early on, before my husband and I were married, I sat with each of my two now-stepdaughters. I told them with full transparency that I was not trying to replace their birth mother. I didn't want them to ever feel they had to choose. I just wanted to be another person to care about, support, and love them. I think that helped us build trust early on when they knew (at least with me) they didn't have to feel guilty about still loving their birth mom and also maybe loving me, which they now do.

Here is some advice from families who shared their stories with us about things they wish they knew:

- Provide as much notice for changes that will affect the co-parent as far out as you can. Planning for several different families who rely on one another is tough, no matter how smooth communication is. The more notice and time you can give the other co-parent(s), the better. Yes, they might use this notice to try and sabotage your plans, but that's between them and their conscience. Err on the side of being proactive to avoid potential conflicts.
- Wait before responding. Sometimes there is a prearranged response time in the divorce agreement, and if so, obviously honor the response time with something such as, "I'm

thinking through this idea and will need a bit more time to process it." If you must respond, give yourself time to de-escalate your immediate emotions. Particularly, if it is a heated conversation, give you and your partner time to talk, prepare a response and work through the communication when you are well-rested, and in a good state of mind not in the middle of your own plans.

- Expect disruptions and even what you perceive as unkindness. Some of the hardest realities as a new bonus parent were events that I was really excited about and had planned for that were met with resistance, changes, and overall dismissal. I'll never forget when a co-parent said that my kids weren't blood so our children had no connections to them and didn't need to be there for important events. After living together as brothers and sisters for many years this hurt and was untrue. However, I picked myself up, communicated honestly how untrue this was and moved on. I trusted that the children knew better and understood that we needed to take the higher road by disengaging. The battle to have someone present can overshadow the actual event and if it does, everyone loses. Keep expectations under control and try if at all possible not to allow disruptions to overshadow the real reason for the celebration/event.

• • •

I always had the same expectations from my stepson that I had for my own children. He didn't understand at that time, being a teenager who had his life turned upside down. As he got older, he thanked me for what I had done for him. He told me, he didn't get it (my expectations) at the time, but now understands.

- Pray. Prayer is my constant companion as a parent and especially as a bonus parent. I remember when my bonus child asked me how I could invite my ex over for holidays and spend time with them. I replied that it was because of prayer and believing that putting our children first was the most important gift to give in this season. Giving yourself boundaries is healthy as well and sometimes I would say, I'd like this to be only our immediate family. However, seek every decision with a thoughtful prayer of how you can be sensitive in the situation, do what you sense is the direction you're being led (not that you like the best) and you'll know you did your very best.

- Give yourself and others the benefit of the doubt. There is a lot going on at all blended families households and giving one another the benefit of the doubt really is important. Although you generally only see a sliver of what their life is like with their other parents, you can assume there are additional struggles, realities and challenges at play. Try to give the benefit of the doubt whenever possible.

"We aren't step or half, we're simply family."
~ M O M S G O T I N K

• • •

I was blessed to become a bonus mom after dating my now husband for three years. During that time I came to love his four children greatly and was a regular part of their lives. I have always felt a strong call as a momma, bringing two children into our marriage and now being a bonus mom to four more.

I was hesitant to meet his kids at first because I knew that I am an all-in type of person. My girlfriend warned me that I was going to fall in love with his kids or they were going to fall in love with me. We were pretty cautious at first, not wanting to rush anything. I actually dressed up as Wonder Woman and went trick or treating with them the first time I met them. Since they were young, they just thought they had a cool super hero with them. This was a win-win because I was able to watch my then boyfriend interact with them, without the pressure of being his girlfriend.

GREAT EXPECTATIONS

There are going to be moments where you question every single part of your decision to become a bonus parent. There will be moments when you wish that you could climb into a dark hole and never come out based on the hurt that you are feeling. There will be words said that will hurt, actions taken that cause pain, or actions taken that cause feelings of being left out. All of this will feel like the worst of the worst.

It's important to remember during the worst of the worst moments, the best of the best moments will surface. Good or bad, these real or imagined expectations can be the most challenging fragments of a blended family. The way we build-up what we think should happen, what each family member needs to act like, look like, and how relationships should be is a trap that we encourage you to avoid.

As we talk through great expectations these were a few of the questions that resonated most with what and how to prepare for becoming a blended family.

- Does documentation exist resolving the big issues with co-parenting?

What is the documented parenting time, holiday plan, maintenance and child support that has been court ordered? Most importantly, remember both parents signed off on these agreements or arrangements. They may or may not have liked the final resolution, but the results were finalized between all parties. Work within these guidelines and if a change is needed, work toward resolving positive changes for the future.

Believe it or not, every aspect of these elements will now impact your life as you step into bonus parenting. No weekday, weekend, or holiday before you were a stepparent will ever look exactly the same after you become a stepparent. Your world will be governed by the terms that were decided on, likely well before you were part of the picture.

Also, for some co-parents, there are no defined guidelines, which can also result in headaches or cause undue stress. Going with the flow or doing it the way it has always been done, even if the court documents direct differently, can work for some very laid-back, incredibly flexible co-parents. But, for most individuals it is a sign that there will be conflict ahead.

To lessen the conflict, get clarity around when the children are going to be with you and when they won't. Gain insight into what issues were so important that they were documented as part of the court order. If the children are older, understand what general rhythms are, how time is split, what financial roles are in play and overall what the relationships look like.

- How will you approach financial issues as a blended family?

In other words, if you know one child will have financial help towards college expenses from a former spouse, do you still contribute the same level of funds you have saved for the other biological child(ren) or do you consider that an opportunity to save money?

What about life insurance policies? How might beneficiaries be divided? Or a Will? Should you consider a Trust? With blended families these issues now become a bit more complex. Especially if you have grown children, grandchildren, a second spouse, stepchildren, or new children. Together, no matter how close we think our families are, we need to carefully plan our estate. Some of the biggest issues that were addressed were when a husband or wife, over time, made a choice to either include or not to include anything to their children from prior marriages or relationships. These are not easy conversations, but necessary and best with full transparency.

- Are there any secrets or important information that is not out in the open? (adoptions, self-harm, addictions, previous marriages, other children, infidelity, etc.)

The last thing you want to do is step into a situation that causes harm for the children and/or yourself. We'd recommend making sure that any secrets are disclosed appropriately based on the child's age before the family goes through another change, meaning you joining it. Use your discretion here and decide how to communicate as a family. For instance, if dad or mom had an affair, that one might be best to hold-up on for a while until the child is older and can handle such a major blow.

However, if it has to do with the child directly, in most cases, we'd recommend that information be relayed before the new family dynamic starts. Also, in most cases, we recommend you being included in these hard conversations so you are part of the parenting team right away. Navigating blended family life is challenging enough, the last thing you need is surprises coming out of the woodwork.

- What if the co-parent is not cooperative?

Unlike the many healthy thriving blended families, there are a large majority of families who are not civil or cooperative with one another. A biological dad may insist that the new bonus dad has no communication with him, or a biological mom may disengage completely and not be involved as much as she once was based on the changed dynamic. Communication may turn ugly, legal, non-existent or be reminiscent of a war. Talking through what the history has been with co-parents will help you know and understand what to expect and plan for.

"Dear Bio Parent: I will not love my stepchild under your conditions, I will love them unconditionally."

~THE SASSY STEP MAMA

- What are the non-negotiables with parenting and what are the differences that occur at each home?

In many cases the two biological parents are somewhat different in the way they parent. Knowing what the significant things like religion, education, traditions etc., they agree and disagree on is step one. Learning what they each will defend in a united way is really important so you can be on the same page. Also, knowing what they have conflicted on previously will help you lessen the chance for stepping on a land mine that you didn't know existed. If you don't know these preferences, it is likely that you'll create problems without even knowing it. By taking on a bonus parent role you are joining the parenting team and knowing the playbook will save all involved heartache.

- What role are the mom and dad hoping you bring as a bonus parent?

First of all, just asking shows respect for an existing dynamic that you are joining. Stepping up as a bonus parent will change your life. Wouldn't you prefer it changes for the better because you understand more clearly what expectations exist?

"You were born with the ability to change someone's life, don't ever waste it."

~UNKNOWN

Some may say many people who are divorced have come from parents who are divorced. This means it is very likely the role of a stepparent has been at play throughout their own history. Knowing what pain a parent carries from their own childhood is very important, so you can avoid bringing that same pain into their adult world.

For one of the families whom we interviewed, this rang very true. The new stepparent had a stepmom growing up who was always there which resulted in having a significantly reduced amount of quality time with her dad. Because of this, when she became a new stepparent, she swung to the opposite direction and was primarily absent in her stepchild's life because she didn't want to infringe on their "solo" time (time just one-on-one with their father). She brought her own experience as a child into her new experience as an adult. While her heart was in the right place for respecting the importance of quality one on one time, this could easily be interpreted by a child that their new stepmom did not want to be around them. Without asking and sharing about why you do what you do, our actions, behaviors or decisions can likely be misunderstood.

• • •

There are psychological effects that divorce has on children. For example; I am always on time and have anxiety when I'm not on time, or when others are late. I relate this to the expectation my parents had on me to always be on time when I was a child waiting for them to pick me up.

As a stepparent you can often be misunderstood, you generally don't have deep roots with the child and so there can be a tendency to avoid or blow up an issue instead of having quality communication and taking time to talk through misunderstandings together.

> *"Behind a lot of great kids is a stepparent who stepped up, stepped in, and gave a sh*t."*
> -~ U N K N O W N

- What are the plans for when conflict arises?

Generally, the question with conflict is not if, but when. Whether it's friction with the children, ex, in-laws or others. Having a plan as co-parents will help to at least talk through what the first steps might be. Agreeing to talk with all parents to ensure there are no misunderstandings about the conflict or having a tool to communicate electronically, maybe the best way. It doesn't mean that just because you have a plan it will unfold exactly that way, but at least you'll be in a better position for preparing your heart and mind. Also, you and your partner should decide how you are going to let it interrupt your day, or how you are going to give it time is important. Make sure you have a plan for how you will defer when you can to protect some moments. Some situations are emergencies, but others are not "drop-everything and handle it right-now" type of issues.

The most important thing to remember is that you are entering a new role with very little information. Taking a step back to understand the history is an excellent way to know how you will move forward as a blended family. Learning what you don't know is a big part of the process, as well as taking queues of what hot buttons are and allowing yourself to listen and decide what your role should be.

If you do have other biological children it's important to know your relationship will be different with your stepchildren. You weren't there for their whole history and so making an effort to understand memories and the past will help them know you are honoring their childhood. If it is deemed appropriate and welcomed, asking children what they want, and don't want as well, can provide helpful insight. It goes both ways.

A feeling of equality with understanding, environment, time, gifts and words will help your biological and bonus children understand they are both very important. It definitely takes extra thought at the time but efforts to be fair in all aspects can return high pay-offs.

If you are new to parenting and your bonus children represent the first time that you will be a parent, learning the environment that you're stepping up for is critical. Reading general parenting books can help but depending on the ages of your bonus children, it may be more helpful to think of yourself as an aunt/uncle. Swooping in too fast can create friction with expectations if they aren't clearly understood by all parents, and even with the children.

• • •

I have been fortunate to have been married to my husband for over twenty-three years. When we were first married, I instantly became a stepmother to three amazing children, one girl and two boys. I was in my mid-twenties and never had any experience with children. I wasn't a babysitter, and I was the youngest in my family. So, if anyone was not prepared, I would say that was me. Looking back, I can only imagine what my husband's ex-wife might have thought when it was his night or weekend with the kids and if I was going to be able to care for her children. Of course, I thought I could do anything – how naive of me to believe I knew the answers.

- Am I ready for all that comes with being a bonus parent? What are my expectations? Is it worth it? Am I ready to give my all for another's child?

This self-reflective gut-check is very important. You are not only adding a new person to your life, likely one you love tremendously, but you are also stepping up to the plate for a role with their children which is hugely rewarding in its own right. It is however, not to be entered into lightly or without intentionality.

Some people will challenge us for adding this question, however, it is truly something that you want to ask yourself, being a bonus parent truly brings you to the reality of selflessness. To a certain degree, it can show you the worst and the best sides of who you are.

The surprise relational pay-off for those who invest wholeheartedly can be absolutely worth every minute. For others there may never be the relationship that they were hoping for and for more still the waves of what it means to their life have not been what they expected.

"Family isn't always blood. It's the people in your life who want you in theirs; the ones who accept you for who you are. The ones who would do anything to see you smile and love you no matter what."

~ UNKNOWN

People often rush into becoming a bonus parent without properly ensuring they know what the commitment will be, without expecting any reward. Only when you are at a place of being about to understand why and what you are doing so you can be all in will you be able to mindfully take the next step.

There's an argument to be made that in some ways being a bonus parent is more difficult than becoming an original parent. There are many dynamics that may make this true, for some but, at a minimum, you should think purposefully about whether you can commit to this new role without any promise of what you'll receive in return other than the assurance of a job well done.

- What will my relationship with my step/bonus children look like?

Fundamentally it's very important to remember that your role in your stepchildren's lives will evolve. It may start with a lot of enthusiasm and then turn into more of a drift once time sets-in, or it may start with distrust and standoffishness, then develop into a solid strong relationship. You will likely have ups and downs with closeness through-out your relationship. Your bonus children may lean on you through a particularly tough time, then they may go a long time without confiding in you. It takes a great deal of self-confidence to know that you aren't the leading mom/dad in their life. Being there for them when they need you, regardless of how long it's been, is one of the fundamental ways that you show them unconditional love.

• • •

What the children decide to call their stepparent can be sensitive. It's smart to ask and never force. If you force a "name" or "title" they are not comfortable with it will cause tension. If it's meant to be it will happen naturally and will have more meaning in the end.

> *"Anyone can be a father, but it takes someone special to be a stepdad."*
>
> ~UNKNOWN

• • •

When we added to our family, that was when everything got interesting. Now we have biological children, stepchildren, and half siblings. I am most proud when people meet our children and assume they are all natural siblings. Unless you really know our family, the assumption is these kids are as close as siblings can be. As I reflect, I believe it was due to our efforts in the success of blending the siblings, but there is some credit that goes to my husband's ex-wife, as she played a key role too. I have never said it out loud (until now) but I need to thank her for the closeness of all five kids. She always supported their children as far as loving their new brothers and was always kind to them herself. She never made her children feel bad when they wanted to talk about their new brothers or prevented them from supporting them. She did a great job stepping up. I have a picture in my home that says, "It takes a village to raise a child." In a blended family we need to be a village.

> *"I was a package deal - something or someone he would have to accept if he wanted my mom in his life. I wasn't a burden in his eyes, I was a bonus."*
>
> ~ASHLEY STOCK

Not all bonus siblings are going to mesh well. Stepping back and letting go of the compulsion to orchestrate all of the expectations and behaviors will keep you from tripping over yourself and hurting your family. Trust and building new relationships take time. They will have the same ups and downs we will experience.

● ● ●

One family shared how they display their family photos. Each family member, as an individual, is framed in their living room and acts like an anchor to remember what's important and why they are doing all that they are doing. All of these photos are strategically placed together on our piano to remind us that we are a family, even though each of us are uniquely different. This simple visual reminds us that each family member has their own place, space, and right to live their own life. We welcome, include, invite, and communicate fairly with each other. At the end of the day, making a family work takes the effort of every single person.

● ● ●

I remember the first time I saw our children really start to bond, and my heart leapt. However, I also remember the first time one of my stepchildren sent a reply to their siblings with very hurtful, unfair words. It's a roller coaster of emotions and it takes time, patience and healing to really build trust. Watching how some of our children, who have put in the effort, have bonded is truly so special but it takes exactly that, them reaching out, trusting and celebrating each other.

Remember, also, that there may be times you feel like everyone is in sync and other times you are having to navigate the same conflicts as before. Keeping a hold of hope will help during these roller coaster moments. Try not to be the doomsday expectation parent who thinks about what the ex is going to say or do, "X, Y or Z." Instead, see the best in that person and keep your expectations to what you can control.

FAIR MAY NOT BE FAIR

Let's be honest, the term "fair" in a blended family can be challenging. Fairness and the inevitable natural hardships of being a blended family make it difficult to keep all tangible and intangible perspectives fair. It's important to keep different viewpoints in mind:

From the **Child's** perspective, is it fair,

- to have to pack clothes each week/day
- to have toys/games at one place or the other
- to have to leave or make new friends
- to have to not be included in activities
- to have two sets of rules
- to be a mediator
- to have to keep feelings inside
- to have to navigate through adult conflicts
- to have two of everything
- to worry about who "will" be or who "won't" be present
- to worry about how they will "fit" into a new family
- to worry about being accepted
- to worry about being acknowledged
- to worry about being loved
- to worry if Stepmom/Stepdad like them
- to worry about upsetting parents/siblings
- to worry about being replaced by new siblings
- to worry about feeling forgotten
- to want attention from their mom/dad
- to feel you may not be able to talk freely

- to feel you may not be able to act freely
- to feel you may not be liked by their own parent(s)
- to wonder if they are loved or even liked
- to feel like they are in the way
- to feel like a burden (financially, emotionally, physically)

From a **Parent's** perspective, is it fair:

- to pay support and not feel it is being applied to the children
- to think attorneys are deciding everything
- to feel like I was the bad person or reason for the divorce
- to have someone else tell me I no longer get my kids or when I get my kids
- to have to split holidays
- to lose joint possessions
- to have to start over in a new home or neighborhood
- to have the perceptions I didn't try hard enough
- to watch my ex be "happy"
- to watch my family, do things without me
- to not be part of my kids' lives all the time
- to not feel in control

From a **Bonus/Stepparent's** perspective, is it fair:

- to know you are a stranger to members of your new family
- to make sure you are always on standby
- to feel you are not in control
- to feel like no matter how hard you try, it is not "right."
- to feel like you are in a race or competition
- to feel judged
- to feel second-guessed
- to feel you are not accepted by friends, neighbors, or family
- to know you tried, but failed
- to know you succeeded, when others wanted you to fail
- to receive very little credit no matter how much you do

Summing it up

For all of our blended families out there, you know all about alternating, compromising and adjusting for holidays and life. Quick reminder to make the best of it, you want a big solid team helping raise your kids and grandkids in a healthy way even if it doesn't mean you always get your way, don't be selfish or threatened, support and be loyal to your co parents, never talk badly about co parents to kids (or anyone really), don't let your kids (or parents, other exes, attorneys) play you against each other, if you have an issue or something seems off talk directly with your co parents, welcome your ex's new loves into the family including them, make room, know there's enough love for everyone and keep your kids out of the bs (no matter how old they are).

KINDNESS MATTERS

When a divorce/breakup or death of a parent happens, the family has changed. As adults, we may seek a new relationship and blend families. As a child, they are at our mercy of trying to adapt to a new environment, different from what they were accustomed to.

Please use this space to journal your thoughts or responses:

_____

_____

_____

_____

_____

_____

_____

"Be the kind of person you needed when you were younger."
~UNKNOWN

● ● ●

I took my stepdaughters to my home when their mother put them in an awful position. I never once talked negatively about their mother. Hearing negative words doesn't do the children any good when they are already hurting.

Interestingly, many people are not open to change, especially adults. We sometimes make a terrible assumption that children are flexible and will adapt. Do they? What sacrifices are made when they are forced to move back and forth? Why are children working with therapists to help them navigate these "easy" transitions? What therapists may be assisting children with is how to deal with the adults in their lives and the changes caused by living in multiple homes. Many benefits can come from blended families, but they shouldn't be expected to be automatic and maybe short-cut the actual transition by rushing change on children.

Understand that it's normal for all parties to go through change differently. For some involved to perceive new rules, expectations, space etc., as unfair, or to be jealous. We don't have to like it but accepting jealousy helps us move forward. I was raised in a traditional family, and I was very jealous of my brother. It is natural. It may seem even more so with blended families because everyone may be fighting or struggling for attention. Focus on the relationships between everyone and find out what each person needs.

Learning about blended families is about to become your part-time hobby because the more you learn from other's experiences, the more informed you will be to create a bonus parent journey that you want.

Stepping back in situations to really reflect on what's important, what's the big picture, what honors the child and your spouse in the situation. These are the ways to avoid the complete let-down of great expectations unfulfilled.

Forgiveness and expectations tend to go hand-in-hand. Recognize that there may come a time when you need to change your expectations to be more realistic about the existing relationships. It's also entirely a-okay to forgive someone and decide that it's unlikely they will be invited into your home again if treated disrespectfully. This is an extreme example, but there are raw situations where it may cause more harm than health to continue pushing towards your idea of what the situation should look like.

We talked about stepping back as the overarching action in this chapter because we often need to reflect and reset to ensure we are painting an accurate picture in our minds. This picture will include what it should be like without taking inventory of what is going on. Everyone wins when we keep our expectations in check, and we usually have a better all-around experience with much less heartache.

BUILDING A SUPPORT SYSTEM

Like the parents, the in-laws have tremendous power over the success or deterioration of a blended family. Which can include your new role in the family. Knowing the dynamics before you meet each person can be helpful. Some were likely big fans of your spouse's ex, and others may have thought they were the worst. Low expectations for relationships, but high hopes, are an excellent way to approach your in-laws. A common theme from those who have been in the trenches is to steer clear of any conversations that lead to gossiping as an intelligent way to navigate.

Some in-laws will seek to bond with you by talking badly about a spouse's ex. This is not a good idea, particularly when there are kids involved. Setting clear boundaries around your commitment to one another and your commitment to not speaking unkindly of the ex can help you and your in-laws navigate better.

Also, keep in mind that your in-laws may continue to have a relationship with your spouse's ex. While most in-laws understand the pain and hardship of the divorce, others aren't as close to their children and continue as if nothing has changed. That was one of the strangest stories we heard while writing this book, where a family member chose only to communicate with their ex instead of her biological son. I highlight this extreme example as a way for you to prepare for just about anything with in-laws.

We heard another story about the bonus mom's brother-in-law passing away that created the perfect storm of why in-laws may want to stay connected with ex-spouses. When he died, his second wife controlled everything, his estate, the children's college funds, etc. While married, she insisted family members not talk to his first wife or bring up anything about her in front of his children. The mother-in-law always insisted on keeping in contact with the mother of her grandchildren just in case something would happen, and so was thankful she did. When he passed away at a young age, her only outlet for her grandchildren was through their mother. We never want to think we may pass away at a young age, but you never know what might happen, and, in this case, had she severed the relationship to appease his second wife, she may not have had contact with her grandchildren. Often when the person who links you to family passes, it's easy for those relationships to fade. When it comes to children, it's the responsibility of the adults to make them feel connected and a part of the family.

As a bonus parent, we need to allow these relationships to exist, as they aren't damaging to our own families. We hope a blended family never places anyone in a position where they must choose one person over another. There is plenty of love in the world. Remember, you don't have to like their past or future partner, but we want to respect their history and future.

> *"There will always be steps you can take*
> *toward unity in your blended family.*
> *You will make it – one step at a time!"*
> ~DONNA HOUPE

Your role is to be kind and supportive to your spouse, which means sometimes laying down boundaries with other family members about how their actions will or will not support your family.

. . .

Several of my in-laws haven't been the most welcoming, which has been a struggle, but my husband reminds me that if he and I are good, everyone else should be as well. I think there is great wisdom in that. I was very stern about fairness and, on more than one occasion, had to have a conversation based on a grandparent bringing only gifts for their biological grandchildren. We were united to say if you can't get all of our children something, don't get any of our children anything. We have plenty, love and time are all they need. We also took a unified front on not allowing the exes to be talked about poorly. This seemed intuitive to us. Still, you can't imagine how many times, particularly in the beginning, we would have to tell a well-meaning family member that we don't talk poorly about anyone in our home, particularly the biological/bonus mother or father of our children.

> *"Live one day at a time (or one moment, if you have to). Blend little by little and celebrate even the smallest breakthrough."*
>
> ~ANDI PARKER-KIMBROUGH

Being a bonus parent should never be a competition regarding position, status, or traditions, as your new family is not a contest. Instead, it's a journey for all involved. I didn't discover this until years later in my marriage to my husband. All parties navigate new roles, relationships, and norms when a divorce happens. We tend to focus on the immediate members or our inner circle, but we must also consider the outlying rings. It takes time for everyone to feel connected.

. . .

I remember when I was first married to my husband, and I was so hurt by my new mother-in-law's comments about her grandchildren. She would say she was thankful to her ex-daughter-in-law for allowing her to see the grandchildren, or because they were being raised Christian, and for most of the positive outcomes of the divorce. The reality was it was because of us she saw her grandchildren more than they did before, and why the children were active in church and for their stronger bond. It was hard not to get angry.

Because time is fluid, so was the healing process for my mother-in-law. It took time and awareness for our families to bond. It took her time to let go of the family that was. It took time for her to trust me through my behaviors and interactions with her grandchildren and other family members. As much as I felt hurt at the beginning by her words and actions, I have come to understand why she said what she said and felt the way she felt. It wasn't anything negative towards me; she didn't know me yet. She knew her son and her grandchildren, and we needed to go through the highs and lows of getting to know, accept, trust, and most importantly, love each other through our own journey. In the end, no one wins a medal. We win when we embrace all involved, the old and the new.

In addition to in-laws, we also recommend building your blended family support system. One child we interviewed said he sought out friends from blended families when his mom was about to get remarried to help adjust to this new life. This is genius. Too often we surround ourselves with people who don't get it because their reality is so different from ours or they are too close to our situation.

Make sure you develop relationships with people whom you can share or vent safely outside your internal circle. Try to establish friendships with other blended families to normalize the challenges you are facing and allow for everyday conversations and to feel grounded.

Remember to stay true to your new partner and family. Trust your instincts; if a relationship is causing a divide in your family, it is likely time to have an honest conversation and set some boundaries to protect your family. Going back to the story, if the grandparents couldn't bring all of the children gifts, they were asked not to bring any of them gifts, this was after the bonus siblings had to watch their brothers and sister receive gifts from their grandparents when there was nothing for the step siblings. This is just unkind and for many blended families a non-negotiable.

While we recognize that there are strong bonds in place, the level of kindness needs to rule here, and if it makes a child feel like they are less than equal, the approach needs to change.

There was also a family where the in-law routinely put down the new bonus parent to their grandchildren, spouse, and ex. This is a perfect example of a time when continuing with the relationship without rules will cause division in the family.

• • •

After I had attended mediation with my ex-wife, something resonated with what the mediator said: "Your child has a completely different relationship with their mom than you have with her, don't confuse the relationships." This helped me because I didn't put my problems with my ex in the middle, causing division between the two or for my issues to be my child's issues.

We loved how one family we interviewed described meeting her sister-in-law's children for the first time—hugging them and loving them just as if they were part of the whole family from the start. Being welcoming and supportive are so important for extended families to understand.

Children are bright, and if you treat one child differently from another child, they will notice. If you, as an extended family member, aren't kind to the child's parent or bonus parent, they will also know. If you are unsure how to navigate the complicated world of exes, new spouses, and new children, we encourage you to talk with the adults in the family to whom you are closest. Express that you want to be honoring all of the individuals in the family and to know how best to do this.

Offering to help a blended family understand how to build a support system is just like helping a traditional family have a conversation. Ask the new spouse if there is anything you can do to help and how they would like you to participate in the event or special occasion. Whether it's watching the kids one night for date night or helping with a meal, be there for them.

As the new spouse, try to make it easy on extended families by sharing likes, dislikes, birthdays, the origin of names, and hobbies the children like. This will help the extended family have some good information to start forming a relationship with their new family member.

"If a family were a boat, it would be a canoe that makes no progress unless everyone paddles."

~ LETTY COTTIN POGREBIN

ALL ABOUT THE CHILDREN

STAND

Keeping you and your spouse/partner's relationship strong is of paramount importance. However, since you have children, there are going to be times where it will be all about the children. When deciding how to settle a disagreement concerning how the family spends its time together, money, gifts for example, we find that settling back and standing on a united foundation is the best way for us to feel good about the direction we're going in. Remember we are on a journey.

An example of how this plays out from one family's story was when the children were older and the ex didn't have a place to go for important holidays, the couple would invite their ex to come spend the holidays with them so they could all be together. This is an example of being all about the children.

There will be times when the child's/children's plans change and your plans will then need to change as well. These are the times when the children will be especially watching for how you adjust and handle the change.

Ask yourself some important questions that place yourself in the child's place. Questions such as: Would this make me uncomfortable? How do I perceive the conflict and how is it impacting me? What would this be like if I didn't have more than two parents? What is a win for the child in this situation? Is the other parent's intention in the right place for the child? Can I compromise to make this situation better for the child?

_____

_____

_____

_____

_____

_____

"Remember why you chose to come together in the first place - the love that you have for your partner. Your partner's children are an extension of them and this makes them just as important to your happiness."

~BETH HAPPINESS

Parents Night is a night where children get to thank their parents for the support provided in their extracurricular activities in school. This night could be at sporting events, musical or special awards given. It is a night that has the potential to have someone feeling left out, hurt, or even unappreciated or unnoticed. It serves as a good example of how to ensure you are thinking about the children first.

How do you handle parents' nights? Today more and more schools or extracurricular activities understand nuclear families in several different ways. However, you may have some old school traditions and again this is a great opportunity to learn when to step up, stand, when to step aside, or when to step down.

For example:

If you know "Parents Night" is coming up, talk with your child about who they want to recognize as his/her parents? We say this because, remember, when a marriage fails often the child has no control in their life or in certain parts of their life, from that moment forward. Remember, they didn't necessarily get to choose who their mom or dad remarried. So, when this is an event that celebrates the "child's" parents, have the conversation.

What if the school will only pay for one rose for their mother? From a child's perception, why make them choose? If they do, it may only make sense to give it to their biological mom. If you are the bonus mom, accept this and try not to make your bonus/stepchild feel bad. This is an opportunity to stand in what you know is right for the child and allow the child's parents to celebrate this moment. Remember it's not personal, it's natural.

If you are a dad, talk with the child about what options that might be available. Here is an opportunity to "step up" and allow your child to celebrate all the moms in their life, if they wish too. Go out and buy the extra roses and make it happen! Try to avoid placing the child in the middle. Let's focus on who the night is celebrating.

• • •

I remember one "Parents Night" with our older son, and it was devastating to my husband. When the announcer read the names only his son's name and his ex-wife's names were announced. My husband's name was not mentioned, but he was right there standing with them. He still walked out onto the field and stood proudly by his son's side.

This wasn't the first time this situation happened. We heard from several families that parents have been left out. At the time this happened the school system only allowed for one address to be primary in the computer system and didn't recognize two separate parental households. Due to the computer system, the coaches only took the primary and didn't think about asking the athletes if they wished to add another parent to the announcement. Looking back, it was a systematic oversight. Our son was hurt, my husband was hurt, it was an awful situation, and it was hard not to think that it was done on purpose. The understanding we have now is so very different. It's all about perspective.

This story shared is significant because we need to be proactive and ask questions as an opportunity to step up! If something goes wrong we need to stand confidently on knowing who we are in our children's lives and not being tempted to play the victim because of an oversight that draws attention away from the celebration of the child.

If you can provide two or more roses, then great! Allow the child to choose whom to give them to, their biological and bonus mom or maybe even a rose to grandma. As the bio parent, again, try not to make your child feel bad for recognizing all the support in their lives. Remember, the village only makes our children stronger.

One of our favorite stories that was shared with us was of a biological mom who whispered to her daughter to give the one rose to her bonus mom. The grace this took was beautiful to see. The mom was secure enough and standing on what she knew would bless her co parent while showing her daughter how to be gracious, thoughtful and generous with honor towards her bonus mom. What a beautiful example and moment.

"The recipe for a unified family: 3 cups love, 1 cup empathy, 1/4 cup patience, and 1 tablespoon teamwork."

~ UNKNOWN

We both have had the opportunity to watch our children navigate getting married, having children, and all the new events that can cause us to be even more aware of all the individuals within a blended family. We found this story that demonstrates how we can always keep the events in their lives about them. Keeping our focus on our children does end once they near adulthood with blended families.

● ● ●

My youngest daughter got married this weekend. Her dad and I are divorced, but we do our best to be on the same page for the kids we share. Granted, they are all adults now, but anyone who tells you co-parenting stops when your children turn 18 does not have children.

Weddings are full of stress and chaos, and our youngest daughter had thought of everything. The wedding was beautiful and went off without a hitch — until it was time for her dad to offer a toast. He starts to thank the guests for coming and then goes totally blank.

Standing in front of 150 guests, I watch him floundering and do my best to jump in and help. I told a story about telling my daughter her time would come and about how grateful we were she had met this wonderful man.

It was an interesting few minutes. But not as interesting as the expression on the wedding coordinator's face about an hour before.

The wedding coordinator pulled me aside and asked, "Who is that woman in the blue dress sitting next to your granddaughter in the front row?"

"Oh," I said, "That's my daughter's father's first wife — her sister's and brother's mother. Her name is Sharyl."

The wedding coordinator's expression was priceless. "What?" she said. "First of all, your ex-husband's first wife is at your daughter's wedding? And, in the first row?"

According to wedding protocol, the first and second rows are set aside for the family. I just shrugged with a laugh. "It's our family. She's my daughter's sister's and brother's mother. She's always been in my daughter's life. It wouldn't be right if she wasn't here."

I must note here that Sharyl and my ex shared equal custody of their children before I came into the picture. The kids went back and forth each week. Sharyl and I developed a friendship because her kids lived with their dad and me every other week and we did our best to coordinate efforts. That's another story. There was a lot of time to build a relationship before my youngest daughter was born — but that meant my daughter never knew a time when Sharyl wasn't around.

All the wedding coordinator could say was, "This is one interesting family."

Is this "normal" wedding protocol? Of course not. But that's the message I have been trying to pass on for years. Second or subsequent relationships do not follow the "normal" protocol. You must stand back, look at what will make your children happy, healthy and secure, and adjust your behavior accordingly. Flexibility and acceptance. That's the essence of a bonus family, and that's good ex-etiquette.
(Blackstone, 2022)

NUCLEAR FAMILY VS BLENDED FAMILY

● ● ●

When our middle son was in high school, I would have never thought his parents' divorce or the fact he had been part of a blended family would ever be a concern. His parents had been separated since before he was one. His life had always been back and forth between households. It changed when his older siblings left for college. Now it was just him and his mother half of the time, and the other half he would come to our home with his father, stepmother, and half-brothers.

Typically, I would have thought nothing of this, but as I reflected, I asked him if it was hard for him to leave his mother's home. Once he left, she was "alone." He felt guilty for leaving her alone, while his father had me and his two younger half-brothers with him. I never understood how he felt, but I do now.

Another observation that was important for us to come to understand was that when he came back to our home there were days he had missed his father, brothers, and I, things we had experienced that he hadn't. So now we are talking about different experiences and he is listening to events he missed out on when he was at his mom's. How could he not feel like an outsider in his own family? I never understood his reality until years later.

We feel this is an important perspective, to be able to place yourselves in their position and try to understand or be aware of how they feel. As an adolescent how does one deal with guilt and lack of belonging. It takes us all back to understanding Maslow's Hierarchy of needs. We all long for safety and belonging. Whether real or not, it is what it is.

• • •

My mom never referred to my half brothers as half, not even once that I can recall. I didn't realize the foundation this made until many years later when I became part of a blended family with half brothers and sisters. The impact that our words and titles make with one another really does show how we feel and how we expect our families to relate to one another. My brothers and I still, now in our middle age, never call one another half and likely never will.

• • •

From the time I was born, my parents always had us call our half-siblings our brothers and sisters. We didn't refer to them or us any differently. So, we were just siblings regardless of where or who we came from. This allowed us to become close, and just like siblings in a nuclear family we learned to love hard and fight hard. We didn't view each other as different or anything special. We were just brothers and sisters.

Try to instill this equality and the power that comes with treating every individual as a part of the collective family. Be mindful of how the child/children are feeling and, as appropriate, ask them to help ensure that a good, safe, loving environment is being nurtured.

LOVE

When we asked parents of blended families what we should include in Stepping Stones, we received an overwhelming response to include a section about Love. Specifically, how to "love" while blending families.

First, we thought we'd introduce you to the different stages and explanations of Love.

The ancient Greeks had four different names for "love." Let's start with Philia, the love of friends. We all may have started our relationship as friends. For couples, when we started dating, we likely formed a friendship before we fell passionately in love with our partner. We also want to identify Phila love for when we first blend with children. We initially formed a "friendship."

From there, we move to Eros, where we experience a passionate love with our partners. This is the love that created our children. Most of us fell in love with our partners and through our love created a new version of ourselves. Reflect on the day your child(ren) was born. Oh, happy day! We never think about this love ending. But alas, here we are. Keeping some of those memories are important because the child needs to know they were born out of love. Which for the majority of us, this is the case. Ignoring or denying that love can bring negative feelings onto your children about how they came into this world. We can honor that we were once in love with their other biological parents with an Eros type of love but then that type of love ended.

Loving our children takes us to a Storge type of love, the love of a parent for their child. When we become parents, we have an instant bond with our children. Maybe, this is why there isn't anything in the world we wouldn't do for our children. Our children are our blood, our DNA, and our legacy. From the moment we meet our children, and grandchildren, we would literally lie in front of a train for them. This type of love is powerful and most immediate. It's important to recognize that your love for your bonus/stepchildren didn't have this immediate birth experience and likely will take time to grow with trust and love. When it does it will likely be closer to a Phila type of love. Still strong, just different.

We also wanted to highlight Agape love, which is the love of humanity. Agape love is love as an action versus an emotion. In blended families, we need to be aware of our actions and the intentions behind them. Think back to the many weddings you have attended or maybe your own and someone read 1 Corinthians 13:4-8.

> "Love is patient; love is kind. It does not envy; it does not boast; it is not proud. It does not dishonor others; it is not self-seeking, it is not easily angered, it keeps no record of wrongs. Love does not delight in evil but rejoices with the truth. It always protects, always trusts, always hopes, always perseveres. Love never fails. But where there are prophecies, they will cease; where there are tongues, they will be stilled; where there is knowledge, it will pass away."
> 1 Corinthians 13:4 -8

> "Agape love is selfless love … the love God wants us to have isn't just an emotion but a conscious act of the will - a deliberate decision on our part to put others ahead of ourselves. This is the kind of love God has for us."
> ~BILLY GRAHAM

Let's break down how we can interpret a lesson from the Apostle Paul as we move forward in fostering positive blended family relationships. Love is patient. Paul wrote this passage while in Corinth, a city known for immorality, wickedness, and dishonesty. In this letter, Paul writes about the power of God's love for all individuals and the community. Love in practice is more about what love does vs. about what love is. You might also hear Agape love referred to as "Love the Verb," as we begin to transform love into actionable intentions towards another person: patience, kindness, humility, forgiveness, trust, hope, and perseverance.

If we are lucky, we can transform this actionable love towards others. If we choose not to love, there can be no true family bond.

Through the phrase "Love is Patient," we are encouraged to embrace a love that is purposeful, persistent, and perspective-driven. We think this is why we wanted to share with all of you how others have succeeded and where we have fallen short.

Patient love is a determined love. It is the kind of love that wives and husbands have for each other. In many of our marriage vows, we may have spoken the phrase "For better or for worse" we chose to be faithful and remain committed to each other, and this commitment is to be long-lasting. Patient love is about the choices we make. We need to choose to love the other person even when we don't feel like it. Many of you are thinking "this is very tough" and that we are asking a lot to call you to choose love; we know it isn't easy. If it were easy everyone would succeed!

Even when you feel someone has wronged you, you should try and love them anyway and not call it quits just because you're exhausted, frustrated, or hurt. Paul wrote that patient love is the foundation for all the other definitions of love.

As blended families, when you have committed yourself to Agape love, remember that love is not self-serving but rather persistent and focused on the well-being of our new family members. We must learn to act kindly towards those we are called on to love. You become more forgiving, gracious, and trusting, regardless of your personal feelings.

Love is kind. Kindness is similar to patience but refers to how we treat each other. It especially implies a love that reacts with goodness towards those who have been ill-treated. Here is where we focus on being kind when others may not be kind to us. Two wrongs do not make a right. It may also be more about picking what is truly important to discuss with necessary parties, verses poking the bear. We know what the results will be if we provoke. Try to focus your energy on kindness.

An excellent resource for understanding how each person receives and gives love differently is, "5 Love Languages" by Gary Chapman. Chapman also wrote the 5 Love Languages for Children, 5 Love Languages for Teenagers, and 5 Love Languages for Men. We've listed additional resources at the end of this book.

Try these love language activities with your new blended family:

- Words: Use words of affirmation, compliment them, give them a card or note in the morning, send a Snapchat or text message, let them know you are proud of them, tell others about their efforts or successes in front of them.
- Physical Touch: scratch their back, rub their hands or feet, have them sit on your lap or cuddle while reading a story, encourage hugs and kisses, start a "high five" routine, go to the mall/spa for a manicure or pedicure/massage.
- Acts of Service: Make doing chores fun with them, teach them how to cook or bake, go out in the garden and plant flowers/seeds, sit at the table and help with homework and be present, help organize their room or unique toys, create a bedtime routine.
- Gifts: Pay attention to what their favorite food or treat is and make it, find out what they like and make sure to give them gifts that represent *their* interests and not yours. Be creative about what they want and see how you can provide a small treat. But remember, you can't "buy" Love. It is not about giving a gift to have them like you, but rather a gift to show you love and appreciate them.
- Quality of Time: Be present. Listen, engage, ask questions. Go for a walk and talk about what you see, how their day was, what they want to be when they grow up, what they

like and don't like. Go out for a special breakfast, lunch, or dinner. Play games and do activities. Do you enjoy a hobby you can do together? Learn to laugh with each other.

With your blended family, the key is understanding each person is special and unique. The above ideas will help you put the scales in better balance. Remember to give yourself grace, and patience. You want to focus on each person as an individual and not the group as a whole.

The Hole in the Fence

"In a small village, a little boy lived with his parents. The boy was quick to anger and taunt others with his words. His bad temper made him use words that hurt others. He scolded neighbors, children, and even his friends due to his anger and everyone started avoiding him. His parents advised him many times to control his anger and develop kindness. Unfortunately, all their attempts failed.

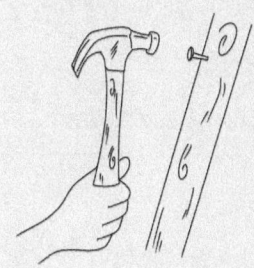

Finally, the boy's father came up with an idea. The father gave him a bag of nails and asked him to hammer one nail into the fence every time he got angry. The little boy found it interesting and accepted the task. Every time he lost his temper, he ran to the fence and hammered a nail. His anger drove him to hammer nails to the fence almost 30 times the first day.

As the days passed, the number of nails hammered on the fence started reducing. The little boy found it difficult to hammer the nails and decided to control his temper. Gradually the number of nails hammered to the fence reduced drastically and the day arrived when no nail was hammered to the fence.

The boy did not lose his temper that whole day and for the next several days he did not lose his temper. So, he didn't need to hammer any nails to the fence.

Now, his father told him to remove a nail each time he controlled his anger.

Several days passed and the boy was able to remove most of the nails from the fence. However, there remained a few nails that could not be pulled out.

The boy told his father about it. Father appreciated that and asked the boy pointing to a hole "what do you see there?". The boy replied, "a hole in the fence."

"Now do you see what your anger does?" asked the father. The boy gave a confused look.

So, the father continued, "The nails were your bad temper, and they were hammered on people. You can remove the nails but the holes in the fence remain. The fence will never look the same. It has scars all over. Some nails cannot even be pulled out. You can stab a man with a knife and say. "I'm sorry." later, but the wound will remain there forever. Your bad temper and angry words were like that!

Words can be more painful than physical abuse. Use words for good purposes. Use words to grow relationships. Use words to show love and kindness in your heart."

The boy realized his mistakes and did not repeat them.

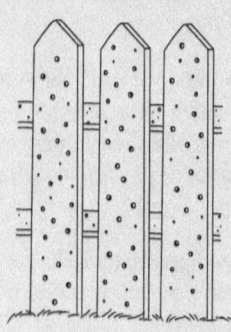

Moral of the story
"Unkind words cause lasting damage. So let our
words be kind and sweet." (Unknown, 2022)

Love does not envy. Love does not boast. Love is not proud. Love does not dishonor others. Love is not self-seeking. How can we appreciate when others are blessed with good things and work hard not to be jealous or resentful? Does it make sense to celebrate our wins and rub salt in old wounds? When we allow ourselves to feel envious, we really bring more ugliness out in ourselves. Love is not angered when others experience success.

The phrase "love does not boast" means "bragging without foundation." Our goal should not be to promote ourselves over others. We should want to take time and recognize everyone's achievements and successes as their own. The goal is to try not to base your own abilities or perceptions from others.

A struggle that we often hear with divorce and blended families is our own characterization of who we are and our own sense of self-importance (or arrogance). We are "now" the new father or mother. We are "now" in a new home, or "now" have new things, etc. What we really want to focus on is how we can use love to demonstrate we care about our new family, their customs, likes, and dislikes. It respects the feelings and concerns of all parties even when they are different from our own.

The feedback we received from families living it wanted others to benefit the most from their past missteps. We should never disgrace or humiliate another person, regardless of who they are. As you enter into a new blended family, help each member to place love ahead of the good of others before your interest.

Love is not easily angered; Love keeps no record of wrongs. Avoid keeping a scoreboard over all the hurts, from the ex-spouses to the stepchildren. Remember, if you are keeping score, so are they. In the end, what does it matter? You are the adult, and they are children.

So often, people say they love each other, but, as soon as one gets angry, out comes the list of everything they have done wrong in the past! The shouting begins and accusations begin, bringing up painful memories about the past. This is not love. Love forgives and refuses to keep track of personal insults received. The focus of love is not one's own pain, but rather the needs of those we love.

Obviously, we should not allow people to continue to hurt us or others. Our understanding is to have the courage to reconcile, and to forgive those we seek forgiveness from and to let go of the past to stay in the present. When we continue to fight over petty items and go to court, who are we hurting? Who is in the middle? How are these actions helping all the people involved?

_____

_____

_____

_____

_____

_____

Love does not delight in evil but celebrates with the truth. Like the characteristic of patience, this kind of love reminds us not to rush towards being angry when others do us wrong. Learn how to let some of the small stuff go! Think about making a peanut butter and jelly sandwich. How many ways are there to make one and who is to say my way is better than your way? Look at what chores are done and how they are done. Does it matter how it was accomplished if the result is achieved?

We think what Paul is trying to explain to us is that love does not hold a selfish concern for one's own rights or ways. We need to be aware that maybe someone was taught or shown differently. This is Okay.

The phrase speaks to the kind of love that offers forgiveness even when we may feel the offenses are repeated many times. It is a love that doesn't keep track of every wrong thing in their eyes our exes, stepchildren, or children do and hold it against them. Let's focus on seeking to avoid involvement in evil and help our family steer clear of evil, too. Let's focus on living and working towards reality.

Love always protects. As parents a primal desire is to protect our family, especially our children. Our goal should be to work with our co-parents in a safe way that won't bring harm, shame, or injury, but relationships that will restore and protect everyone involved. Referencing back to the "Hole in the Fence" story, our actions and words have consequences. "You are protected, in short, by your ability to love."

• • •

I was always in a good place with my in-laws, and they accepted me into their family. When we were first married it was great, we had time together, just the two of us and then time with the children, kind of the best of both worlds. What I loved about my husband the most was that he placed fatherhood first and being a husband second. I know this may sound odd, but remember, his children were before me and I knew and embraced his love for his children. I would not have had it any other way.

Love always trusts. Allow time for trust to evolve. Especially when reflecting on the ages of the children involved. Depending on the circumstances of the new relationship it takes different amounts of time for individuals to trust each other. When trust has been broken, and depending on the emotional attachment of the trust, we must allow time and actions to be present. Sometimes we need to allow for the benefit of the doubt, allow us to see the best in others, and trust in their good intentions.

Love always hopes. No one goes into any marriage or relationship anticipating a divorce or parting, we always have hope. Allow yourselves to hope for the best where others are concerned. This hope filled love encourages others to press forward in the faith that we can be successful in blending our families. We are going to have high and lows. Marrying for the second time (or more) has more challenges.

Statistics show that in the United States, 50% percent of first-time marriages, 67% of second marriages, and 74% of third marriages end in divorce. (Pope, 2018)

Some reasons marriages after the first still end in divorce because of divorce baggage, remarrying for the wrong reasons, not spending time getting to know their partner, the children, multiple marriages may have stepchildren, the ex-factor, money, and existing family matters and in-laws. We need hope. Love always hopes.

Love always perseveres. This kind of love endures even through the most difficult trials.

Love never fails. In the context of a marriage or partnership, even when we are unfaithful or unloving, God remains faithful and patient. God's love is constant. It's this kind of love he challenges us to have for others. We must learn to love our new families.

Paul's encouragement of being patient in the love for each other and patient in the love we show for others. If we can be patient and committed to loving our new entire family, we create unity, purpose, and strength. When we adopt a patient love for our new family, we can see all members as precious and a gift. This kind of love goes beyond the boundaries of ordinary love. It is eternal, divine, and will never cease.

What is going to be my go-to when things get really challenging?

_____

_____

_____

_____

_____

_____

Likely you have coping skills for stress today, the goal would be to have a plan for healthy skills once you are in this new role as well. Remember that time passes, emotions fade and at the end of the day the most important element in your control is how you respond and how you cooperate. We know it can be frustrating to feel as if you are always the one taking the high road. In the end though, your children are watching and learning what it means to deal with people they don't necessarily get along with. This is a vital skill in every single workplace and home in the world. There may come a day and time where you take the higher road surfaces in an apology, act of appreciation and overall being honored for communicating kindly and cooperating well. Know this though, even if that day never comes, you will sleep well knowing you are doing everything you can in the situation.

"Family is a lifejacket in the stormy sea of life."
~J.K. ROWLING

How many of you have either read the books or watched the Harry Potter movies? Love is the theme throughout the entire narrative. A mother's love was the unbreakable spell used to save her son from Voldemort. Harry's love for his friends protected them in the final battle between good and evil. Professor Snape's love of Harry's mom, Lilly, caused him to safeguard Harry all those years. Professor Dumbledore reminded Harry, "To have been loved so deeply, even though the person who loved us is gone, will give us some protection forever." Dumbledore emphasized how the power of love conquers all.

How will you choose to love?

AWARENESS OF BLENDED FAMILIES BASIC NEEDS

We must think about how children feel when there is a disruption in their nuclear family. What we found insightful was the awareness children have regarding their "role" in a blended family. To understand this perception more we found ourselves going back to Maslow's Hierarchy of Needs. The basis of Maslow's Hierarchy begins with how physiological needs are met for each person. These basic needs are food, water, sleep, clothing, and a home. (MasterClass, 2020)

One of our respondents wrote that she felt like she didn't belong in either household when she was young. When we first read this comment, our hearts sank. We don't believe any person intentionally wishes or wants a child to feel left out. But here is the cold hard truth: sometimes we choose to ignore our opportunity to take a stand and focus on how to provide a home with not just physical warmth but emotional warmth as well. How might you allow your/their home to reflect a sense of belonging?

When children are under the age of 18, after a divorce they typically go back and forth between their parents' homes. Imagine spending your childhood having to make sure you have all of your clothes, personal items, homework, toys, or other activity equipment with you each time you move between homes. Then, while at the other household, you "forgot" something! How do you think those conversations started?

"Mom, I left my _____ *at Dad's house. Can we go back?"*
Think about how **you** might or did respond:

> *"I am not going back to your dad's house. You're*
> *just going to have to deal with it."*

> *"You'll have to call your father, and maybe he will bring it over."*

> *"Well, I will try, but I have other things to do;*
> *you need to be more responsible."*

> *"Sure, let me call your father to see if he is home, and*
> *we'll make arrangements to get your* _____."

> *"Let's not worry about this, we'll just have a new* _____."

> *Or maybe your body language spoke, did you ...*
> *Roll your eyes*
> *Laser beam eye stare*
> *Use the dramatic heavy sigh*
> *Turn your back and walked away*
> *Throw your head back with arms in the air*
> *Gave a reassuring smile and a wink*

Now, depending on how often a child may forget an item(s) is neither here nor there. When everything is in one place, it's much more accessible. When they go back and forth between homes, we must help them manage expectations and additional stress. Each time they pack a bag and head to the other house imagine what might be going through their mind?

We should think like we're packing for vacation. How often do you forget something when packing for a vacation? I have yet to "remember" everything. Some of the items often overlooked are the "no brainers." Why? Because we're excited! Not saying children are not happy about seeing their other parents; it's different. How would you adapt to living your life out of a suitcase? Packing bags each week or every few days gets old; trust me, it's not a "vacation," it's everyday life.

Would you ever think "food" would be a concern? Who is going to pay for school lunches? What does the divorce agreement state? What if they don't want school lunch and wish to have the al la carte lunch, or maybe leave campus for lunch or school snacks are brought from home? Who would ever have thought that "food" could become a significant issue? Well, it does and how do you think these back-and-forth conversations affect the young ears listening in? What are they feeling?

Here is a classic situation. The teacher sends a note "home" stating your son/daughter is almost out of snacks; please send more. Which home takes care of the snacks? Is the teacher supposed to have this written down, is the child supposed to know Dad does the milk and the first half of the year lunches, then mom makes the snacks and takes care of lunches the second half of the year? Oh no, now the ex is upset because they have to go and pick up snacks. We just don't understand why the adults get upset, mad, or flustered in these situations. More importantly, what is the effect on the children listening to the bickering back and forth?

Really? Don't let the small stuff take away from what is essential. Stand in the gap and make it a non-issue because the only person who suffers, typically, is the child. Soon they will stop asking or stop talking. They will begin to feel any request will blow up into a big issue. Later in the "Give yourself and others Grace" section, we'll learn to use the 10-10-10 Rule. This is a great example of when to use this tool to help everyone "reset" into the right mindset. We have a choice here. Let's focus on what is right.

"Establishing living arrangements is an important part of setting up a blended family, and it plays a big role in how well your stepchildren will adapt to their new home life."

~ ELIZABETH BRYANT

Now imagine your step/bonus child at your home. When we are a guest at someone's home, we typically will wait to be offered something to drink or eat. I can't imagine walking into someone's house only to open up the refrigerator and start pulling meat, cheese, and mayo out to make a sandwich. Or open the cupboards or walk in the pantry and start foraging for snacks. We only do this in our own homes or with close family members or friends. But for stepchildren, some may feel as if they are guests in the homes of their mother or father. Their "home" no longer exists.

Ask yourself, have you granted them permission to be comfortable in your home either through actions or words? Do they reach out for a bite to eat on their own, have a space where they can hang, or even toys or games that are their own? There might be an assumption that children are adaptive and will get used to the new schedule, home, routine, etc. Do they? When blending families, we need to start at the foundation and have a good solid base. We have also heard from many respondents that we need to give this time. Time may be a few months or longer. Trust the process. Allow it to happen organically.

Clothing budgets also tend to be a hot topic for many blended families, what one household spends on clothes vs. the other. Will parents divide the cost? Who decides on the budget or the clothing needs of the child/ren? Then there are the items that you begin to have two of everything, one at each home to make it easier for that spur of the moment activity such as going to the pool or sledding! We should step back and look at the situation from a different lens, and we can recognize the importance of having an open communication plan with all parties.

Once we have the foundation set, we need to create safety. Children need to feel protected. Again; our focus in this book is not about abusive or violent parent situations. We hope that anyone would do what they need to in order to protect any child and remove them from a dangerous situation when necessary. Instead, our focus is on emotional stability and wellbeing. How do you, as a stepparent, step up and engage in these new relationships? Are we trying to get to know our stepchildren and converse with them as if they are our own? Grace and time are requirements for you to understand as you get to know each other.

_____

_____

_____

_____

_____

_____

Another factor to be aware of is the financial capacity of both parents. Once there was a household of possibly two incomes, or perhaps a parent was a stay-at-home parent. Now there is a divorce and maybe a remarriage. The parent who stayed home now has a full-time job, some new bills like daycare, rent, insurance, healthcare needs, etc. Yes, there may be an agreement in place as to who pays what, the amount of child support provided, tax deductions, and so forth. But the change in overall financial situation creates stress on the parents, thus stress on the child.

At what point do you explain to the child and how much do you explain? What do they need to understand without bringing them into an adult situation? You may have to look at a simple need vs. wants plan. Universal feedback from existing blended families, is to avoid blaming the child for their money woes. Be proactive and step in regarding solving these problems.

The challenge is when any level of this hierarchy is not met, it can cause a disruption in personal growth for any individual (adult or child). As bonus parents, fostering the environment for development is essential for your relationship and so much more for the child. When the needs are met, we experience change, but we tend to stay stagnant or regress when these needs are deficient. Divorce is often the disruption to stunt a child's underlying need to feel part of their family.

"In family life, love is the oil that eases friction, the cement that binds closer together, and the music that brings harmony."
~ FRIEDRICH NEITZCHE

In Maslow's Hierarchy of Needs, the third phase is providing love and belonging. If you have successfully delivered the first two stages, we can focus on how we love. Earlier we spent a lot of time discussing love and its different forms. As a stepparent, we have an opportunity to develop a new door in understanding love and belonging within a family.

As humans, we long for connectedness with one another. One article we found stressed the importance of putting the children first! All families have struggled through many current affairs (socially, politically, economically, etc.). We have seen an uptick with more anxiety with blended families during these challenging situations or just a change in general. The key is for all parents to work together.

"The more co-parents communicate with one another about the children, the less likely small issues will grow into major problems."
~ RECITETHIS.COM

- *Keep communication open. Answer all forms of communication (phone calls, texts, emails, etc.) with your co-parent promptly. Give yourself time to think if you are tempted to respond too abruptly. Don't keep score.*
- *Enter each conversation with finding a solution together as your goal.*
- *Stay socially connected while physically distanced. Schedule virtual catch-up calls between your co-parent and your child. Set a time and make the child available for video calls.*

- *List who's responsible for what on each day, week or month. Select days/times for phone, email or in-person visits. Discuss, in advance, visitation, or transfer agreements.*
- *Once this crisis is over, set aside extra time so that the non-custodial parent and child can become comfortable together again.* (David Hill, 2022)

• • •

One big issue that we had was how chores were completed in the household. My wife, the biological parent, did not have her children' doing chores around the house. Yet, we both grew up in houses where our parents required us to do chores. This became a hot issue at times when chores were assigned.

"Remember, this too shall pass. The good, the bad, the ugly - don't get too attached to any one feeling. Also, use a chore chart, for the love of all that is good in the world. Seriously, it changes everything."

~ RAIYE ROSADO

The overall theme is for the family to stay connected. We live in a time where technology makes FaceTime/video chat easy. Invest in phones, tablets, echo show, or whatever technology is appropriate for your family. Be creative in how you engage with your blended family. If something exciting happens at your house and it's one of those events your stepchild wants to share with mom or dad, let them! Please encourage them to want to be connected and support their space.

STORMS - COMMUNICATION IN ACTION

STEP ASIDE

"The secret to blending families is—there is no secret. It's scary, and awesome, and ragged, perfect, and always changing. Love and laugh hard; try again tomorrow."

~ MIR KAMIN

What are storms? During conversations with individuals regarding their blended family experiences, we found that "storms" occurred throughout their journey. In a blended family, these are the situations within a typical family that may be nothing or cause a sprinkle. Typically, nothing major like who is going to pick up from practice or a change in weekend plans.

In a blended family, these situations may turn into full-force severe weather because of all the forces of nature swirling against each other. Sometimes these storms occurred right at the beginning of the relationship when the biological parent felt intimidated by the new bonus parent and flexed their new role within the family right away. For others, the start was more welcoming and turned into ongoing battles.

For a few unique families, they were able to keep storms at bay through mutual respect and inclusion. These are the families that really do it well. Keeping your head and remaining calm when storms come isn't the most instinctive response but is the best advice.

One family we met shared an experience about a heart breaking message they received from the biological parent just days before the couple's wedding, saying that the biological mother was not going to be part of a parenting team with the new bonus mom. This was in stark contrast to another story we heard of a biological mother taking the initiative to host her ex-husband and his soon-to-be new wife into her home to talk through co-parenting together before the wedding.

We highlight these two examples because it's important to be prepared for anything. You do not have control over how your new spouse's ex is going to behave towards you. The hard part is however the exes behave is directly related to how their children may determine how they engage and treat you.

"One of the most important lessons our children have learned from divorces is that some things in life can come to an end, but that's okay because something new is manifested. In our case, it's a blended family that has respect, love, trust, authenticity, and a sense of fun."

~JENNIFER KESSLER

Communication can be especially tricky during storms. Keeping the conversations flowing between your spouse and their ex is often the best strategy. Unless you are asked by either of them to be involved, it is smart to keep your distance.

● ● ●

I was lucky in my situation as both my husband and his ex-wife are great parents. They just didn't work well together. But even the best parents have challenges. What may have been a non-issue while married is now a discussion on what foods the children will eat, who is able to be a babysitter other than the parents, what clothes the children will wear, what activities the children will participate in, who picks up or drops off and so forth. As another "voice" in the conversations, I realized that these conversations were best for them to work out and my input was not needed every single time. It was necessary for me to know when to "step in" and when to "step out."

Watching what you say, or "text," during these amplified storms is even more critical than during calmer days. While it might not be fair, if you are careless with your words, they will be remembered and likely thrown back at you in future storms, or worse in mediation or court.

Court or no court this is the fundamental question that pops-up when the storm has raged seemingly out of control. If you can avoid court, with all of the tension, expense, headache and stress it brings, by all means do. However, if your relationship with your child is suffering due to false allegations, loss of parenting time, financial hardships and there is something to be righted that the other co-parent is not willing to right without court, this may need to be the path you take.

"The hardest thing about being a blended family is knowing when to fight and when to let it go."

~ANONYMOUS

• • •

I was raised in a blended family for as long as I can remember. Throughout the time I spent in the blended household I never got along with my stepparent, now as an adult, I don't have a relationship with my parents due to this issue. I have tried numerous times to have a relationship with my parents, but my stepparent gets in the way and makes everything about them. So now, I have just given up. The mental capacity it takes to deal with an energy-sucking stepparent is not worth the minor happiness I receive spending the limited amount of time with my biological parents.

The story above highlights that the relationship you want with your stepchild/ren may never become a reality. This doesn't mean that you should stop being kind or approaching them with openness towards a better relationship. However, sometimes our personalities just clash and the outcome is that there isn't the level of harmony you wish there was.

Accidents happen! Whenever a child is hurt parents are always on high alert, but when there is an injury within blended families this can sometimes turn into a EF5-tornado! We wanted to add these moments to keep us all grounded:

● ● ●

"Our son, who was about 9 years old at the time, had fallen off a tree and broke his wrist. His older half-sister was hysterical and asked if he was going to die! We didn't know if she was truly concerned about him or if maybe wishful thinking?"

● ● ●

"Our son was at his bio-mom's house playing hockey with some friends when he was hit in the forehead with a hockey stick, his mother, of course took him to the ER, but also needed to go to work, so here I am as the stepmom tag teaming at the hospital. As soon as I got into the room the doctor was numbing his head so they could put stitches in. Once he removed the needle it was like they turned on a fountain and blood started to stream out, I went on the floor! I passed out and my stepson explained to the medical staff, "That was cool, my mother would have never done that!"

● ● ●

"I remember telling my son to be careful and not fall off the boat, and as soon as I said it, he fell, so off to the hospital we went to get stitches and I dreaded the conversations I was about to have with my ex. We just need to remember that accidents happen. Scars are cool and this could have happened anywhere. It's easy to place blame when it's not you, but remember karma, accidents can happen at any time."

How might you prepare for potential storms? What thoughts do you have to create a plan for when these storms pop up?

_____

_____

_____

_____

_____

_____

GIVE YOURSELF AND OTHERS GRACE

I once saw a meme that said something like "I can't wait to grow up to be a Stepparent!" said no child EVER! Who really wants to sign up for that role? Well, we would not have it any other way. While talking about having grace, I opened up my fortune cookie for the night's Chinese take-out only to have the message say, "If you are never scared, embarrassed or hurt, it means you have never taken chances." There will be times in which you are going to be scared, embarrassed, and hurt. Embrace the role and celebrate the many highs...and lows.

Many of our respondents talked about having "grace" when we sent out our survey. Grace is a term we are hearing more and more these days. Maybe it's because of recent events, the current political environment, or maybe people are just feeling the need for more kindness in the world. Grace is the act of showing kindness to someone else even when they may not deserve it. Wow, what a powerful concept. Grace means going out of our way to demonstrate compassion, kindness, and even love (agape) to someone who may not want, appreciate, or return those same feelings or actions.

How can we provide insight on giving you permission to "step up" to look for opportunities to allow "grace" in your relationships within your blended family?

Maybe we need to start with "why" we would want to extend grace onto others. It takes us back to our early teachings of God's love for all people. Even in the coldest of hearts, God never stops loving us. God never quit us. God steps up and shows us the way to step up when needed.

Maybe we can contribute all the good that has come to us through the "Grace of God." How many of you have said this phrase? Now think about this grace with our blended families. Often, I think we are getting by on a "wing and a prayer." But in all honesty, I have prayed a lot! Prayed to be a good role model, a cheerleader, a friend, and another strong branch on our family tree. I prayed for us to be happy, normal, and healthy. No one wants to fail.

• • •

"I often get, "You look so young for having five children!" In which I responded, "Pregnancy, labor and delivery was incredibly easy, all I said was "I DO," and I instantly became a mother of three!"

• • •

"I relate my journey on navigating my blended family like I grew up eating Italian and now I am eating Chinese! Both GREAT, just different."

Are you starting to think, "Enough already, share with us how you extend grace to others!" Yes, we are getting there. We want to stress that showing or giving grace does not mean you are a doormat; you are not giving in. No one should be a doormat or give up, but allow us to provide you with some practical tools to use. Okay, here we go.

Grace through Forgiveness

> *"Do not take life too seriously. You will never get out of it alive."*
> ~ELBERT HUBBARD

Forgive our children/spouse/ex-spouse because they know not what they say or do. Sometimes I wonder when we start to blend families why we all tend to act like two-year-olds. Think about it, have you ever met a two-year-old who didn't want to get their own way? They are master manipulators. What our focus should be on is how we can forgive to move our family forward. To heal, to be happy, and to be healthy. Rehashing the past only allows us to live in the past. We can learn from our past to allow our future to be new.

I spoke with one young lady, whose parents were never married, about how she traveled back and forth between both her mom and dad's homes on weekends. Each time she was dropped off by her mother she said she cried. Whenever we see tears, we naturally tend to believe she is feeling sad, upset, hurt. Imagine what her mother was thinking when she drove her daughter to her father's home, and she cried? Imagine what her father was thinking about having his daughter crying when she saw him? Now imagine what she was feeling as a four or five-year-old crying in front of both her parents?

As she talked about her reaction, she said to me that she really didn't know why she cried, only that she did. It wasn't because she was going to miss her mom, or that she didn't want to be with her dad, but rather just a reaction she had. Her father has since passed and she reflected on the guilt she now feels about those weekends. She often wondered what her dad was thinking or feeling, and all she was thinking, and feeling was "I love you daddy."

No child or spouse wants to be part of a divorce. We don't wake up in the morning and raise our hands and shout out "I can't wait to break up my family today!" We yearn to have a healthy, happy, normal family. And yes, sometimes we do end one version of our family to try again. There is no simple formula, other than trust, forgiveness, and love. When we don't forgive, we are only holding ourselves back.

> "There is no such thing as a 'broken family'. Family is family, and is not determined by marriage certificates, divorce papers or adoption documents."
> ~ C JOYBELL

If you ever watch the series Mad Men (not the best example of family, but hey, we are talking about divorce, remarrying, and blending) there is a scene in which Betty Draper invites her ex-husband Don to celebrate their youngest son Gene's birthday. Betty's girlfriend is curious and asks her why she was allowing Don to attend their son's birthday party. Betty responds, "I have everything." In her mind she was able to move on with her new husband, in her home, with her children, and sees that by not allowing all the flaws of their marriage to interrupt his relationship with their children. It wasn't about her, but rather an opportunity for them to step up!

Grace with the use of our Thoughts and Words

We often replay in our heads the times we wished we had learned to reframe our words. Words can either lift or tear down a person. How might you be more conscious about the words you use or choose to describe your family, the children, or others?

When we start to use our emotions to drive a narrative, we can let our emotions get the best of us. Here is where we need to take a step back and think about what is happening in the moment.

Take a moment to reflect on a real-life example in which your emotions took control of your behaviors and caused you to do or say something you later regretted?

What was the situation?
What were you feeling?
What did you say or do?
What were the consequences?

Did you know our brains think with two systems? The first system is fast thinking and is involuntary and automatic. It allows us to turn our heads when we hear someone call us by our name, it's instinctive. The second system is slow thinking, and it takes self-control to process through a situation. We all react and then later go...whoa... what was I thinking? The reality is we weren't thinking, we experienced an emotional trigger. It's going to happen.

Becoming more aware of these moments is a skill we wished we often had when we were first blending our families. Taking a moment to reframe your thoughts and words will go a long way in fostering new relationships with all the key players. We need to think about what was said or done that set us off. Then we need to seek to understand "why" what was said or done "is" an emotional trigger?

Sometimes it's because of our past experiences, how we were raised, taught, or stories we heard. Sometimes these beliefs are real and sometimes they are imagined or assumed. What were your actions once you were triggered? What was your response? What about the other person? Lastly, how might the emotional conversation be averted? What do you need to step back to understand? Sometimes we need to recognize another's point of view. Maybe we just need to step away and take a short break. Allow yourself grace and patience. We may or may not agree, but focus on working on acknowledging where the other person is at.

For example:

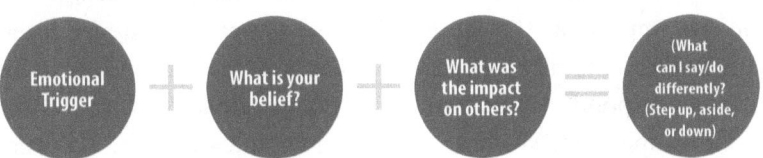

Emotional triggers are the feelings, events, or conversations we have with anyone that elicit an emotional response. Our emotional responses can be rational or irrational. When an emotional trigger happens, we either go into system one thinking and respond quickly which may be ok or cause a storm. Or you can go into system two thinking and delay the response to think the situation through, to find a new path to avoid the storm.

What might be some Emotional Triggers:

- Feeling like you are being unfairly judged or treated
- Chores assignments within the family, fairness

- Rewards/Punishments
- Money
- Schedules

What is your belief? Our own belief systems are based on who we are. Basically, our beliefs are influenced by our own childhood, education, experiences, relationships, and upbringing. What we believe is our own reality.

So here are some examples of what your belief system maybe:

- *All stepparents are not real parents, they don't understand, care, or are only concerned with "xyz."*
- *His/her children get ___ with my children get___.*
- *His/her children are so spoiled!*

The part that many of us who have been living in blended families have learned the hard way was how to step back and reflect on the impact on the family. Because stepparents, stepchildren and other stepfamily members are viewed differently, the results of how we respond to situations that create potential conflict become a bit complicated. We have to stop and think about the potential consequences whether we want to or not.

Example of what the impact might be on others:

- *I became defensive or argumentative and angry. The children stop listening, feel threatened, and shut down or lashed out. We no longer communicated. More arguments.*

The discipline to practice the skill to think how you can communicate towards a positive outcome or react in a way that is perceived as fair as all. In this practice is where you discover how to step up, step aside, step down or to stand still.

Understand what can I say or do differently? (Step up, aside, or down)

Recognize the value of subjective beliefs systems and the fact it may not be able to be eliminated. Seek to understand the child's, coparent, ex-spouses' true intentions and feelings, what is their reality. Take away information that is valuable for you and throw away what is unimportant without becoming angry or defensive. Remember to balance your desire for fairness with their interest in preserving the relationship.

"Blended families are a beautiful mix of diverse people who each serve an important role in our lives. At times, it can be challenging to appreciate everyone's unique beauty."
~DEANA KELLER LA ROSA

As we begin to recognize some of the triggers that lead us into challenging situations, let's now focus on reframing some of our words and thoughts to work towards a better way to communicate. Here is a simple exercise to help you reframe some of your words or thoughts you have about others. How can you turn words or questions that can hurt into words or questions to foster a healthy relationship?

Avoid Asking/Stating:	Start Asking:
Why are you being so difficult?	*What can I do to support you?*
Why can't you just do what I tell you to do?	*Tell me how you have been taught to do this …*
You are so spoiled.	*How have you done this before?*
Don't you know how to do anything?	*May I show you? Can we do this together?*
Why do you always take their side?	*Help me understand what the history was?*

I know I am not your mother/ father!	*How did your mother/father make/do this?*
That's your mother's/father's fault!	*What is the new schedule?*
I'm not talking to you!	*Can I give you a call back in 30 minutes?*
I don't need to tell you what I spend, you need to pay your half.	Jimmy/Jenny would like to …and we agreed we would support this, can we both split this?
I am bringing the children back a few hours later, and will be there at 7 pm.	Would you be okay with me bringing back the children at 7 pm? I would really appreciate a little extra time if possible.

Grace by Letting Go!

We like to introduce you to our version of the "10-10-10 Rule." Maybe you have read 10-10-10 by Suzy Welch as she takes you through transforming your life by reviewing the consequences of our decisions in 10 minutes, 10 Months, and 10 years. (Welch, 2006) Most resources use this method to make better decisions, we are using this rule to help us put in perspective what is important and what we need to let go of. Sometimes when we get hung up on an issue, we step back and think about these questions:

- Is this going to matter in 10 minutes?
- Is this going to matter in 10 hours?
- Is this going to matter in 10 days?
- Is this going to matter in 10 weeks?
- Is this going to matter in 10 months?
- Is this going to matter in 10 years?

If my response is yes to all, then the topic is something pretty important that needs to have further discussion. If I answer yes to the first question then no to the rest, then this may be a situation to let go.

Here's how we put this rule into practice: Your ex-spouse calls and tells you "Jimmy" needs $1,500.00 to pay for books for school. You have an agreement in place, but this is outside of the agreement, and you don't have the means to pay all or even half right now. What do you do?

We start by asking these simple questions, is this going to matter...depending on the response it helps direct the conversation.

Is it worth the battle? Yes, no, or maybe? It's necessary to reflect on what is truly important. What if the situation was, my ex-spouse calls and says "Jimmy" needs $1,500.00 to pay for a ticket for Spring break in Daytona, Florida and we're not paying, but since you no longer pay support you can. How might you respond?

Sometimes it's actually shocking what the topics are that we can debate, particularly with exes. We have even heard arguments over how clothes or towels are folded. WHAT?! We found this example of different way most people fold towels.

So, what kind of towel folder are you? Do you roll your towels, fold in thirds, or fourths, or do you simply hang it up? Can you believe how one folds a towel sparked a huge debate on Twitter? In all honesty, how we perform some of the simplest tasks will create huge battles that are not needed.

Personally, we grew up folding towels like in example one, in quarters, it's how our mother folded towels. Then when I married my husband, he informed me that the proper way to fold towels was in thirds, as this is how his mother showed him. Currently we fold towels depending on which bathroom linen closet they are going in. In our guest bathroom the towels are rolled, for the children's bathroom (if the towels actually make it in the closet) are just thrown up on the hook, and in our master bathroom towels are actually folded in thirds. Four ways to step up, step down, and step aside. Everyone is happy!

Now we totally understand that some of us are wired to be very organized. In fact 45% (NCTI, 2022) of the population tends to have organizational tendencies and they appreciate order, schedules, and procedures. While another 40% (NCTI, 2022) of our population is the complete opposite. No wonder we have conflict! What if I like to have my socks folded together and my husband likes to have them just thrown in the drawer or better yet a basket! WHAT? Now go back to the 10-10-10 Rule. I am going to say, "WHO CARES!" Focus on what is meaningful and what works for how an individual is wired. Some of us like to be organized, God bless you. And some of us like to be spontaneous, God bless you. Some of us are somewhere in between, God bless you as well.

Each household has rules. Keep those rules simple and keep them consistent along with any consequences. Here is where we need to let go of any assumptions we have regarding all parties involved. For example, "I always have to be the heavy," or "You just want to be their best friend." Come to a collective agreement as to how children are going to be punished and agree on the consequences. Remember, you may not get your way, but please meet in the middle. Likewise, if there are other children in the household try and keep to the same agreement to keep fairness when possible. If not, then provide transparency. Let the others know "why" there is a difference. Remember, life is not fair and we need to work to try to keep balance as much as possible. Let's step up!

How do we support fairness in blended families? This might be the golden ticket question. "Fair" is so personal as to how each individual perceives it. The balance to ensuring the right approach takes intentionality and conversation. There could be a child thinking, "Oh, this is awesome, I get two birthdays, holidays, more vacations, etc.!" Then there could be a child thinking, "Why don't I get two of everything?" Life isn't fair and it likely won't always be perceived as fair. But, we can be more aware of the scales and do our best to try and balance them whenever we can. Just being mindful of keeping things fair and keeping the dialogue open is moving towards the right direction.

What happens when we don't get our way? Again, think about the 10-10-10 Rule. Does it really matter? I had plans with my girlfriends for a girl's night out and my husband's ex-wife calls and asks to switch because of a last-minute event. Now, I'm going to be late because I have to be home for an hour and a half until my husband can be home. Will my friends understand being a little bit late? Maybe this event is a vital meeting for her about a promotion or a big sale? Maybe it's simply a favor. Keep in mind, all the children will remember that it was an ordinary day and you were home. Compared to a "big" argument over having to rearrange plans. Who gets hurt? The children. It's like an episode of Project Runway, just make it work.

"No family is perfect ... We argue, we fight. We even stop talking to each other at times. But in the end, your family is your family. The love will always be there."
~ U N K N O W N

Be Realistic

Boy, if there were ever two words, we wished we had been told before becoming a bonus parent they are "Be Realistic." Take a moment to have grace and set realistic expectations. Oh wait, there are no realistic expectations! Wouldn't it be great if there was a book titled, "What to expect when you marry a Man/Woman with one boy and one girl, no wait, two boys (three years old and six years old) and three dogs, wait we need to add my two girls (fifteen years old and seventeen year old) their hamsters, and a partridge in a pear tree.

What we really need is a book buffet in which you can select the sections that work for you and your family. One section for how long you had been married, another for how long you have been divorced, one for if you have children, one for no children, then a section for each age and sex of the children, one for religion, or one for no religion, and so on. Hey, we might be onto book two here. New York Time Bestseller List, here we come! No matter what the reality is we still must be realistic in our expectations.

At first, I tried to provide the image of a perfect family. Everything is "great," the children are "perfect," all the adults are on the "same page." The reality was, "who's fooling who?" Now, our joke in our family is we say we have plenty of faults, and if anything, have given our children a lot to discuss in therapy. They will definitely get their money's worth. We try to be lighthearted when possible. We're glad that we weren't normal. Normal can be boring, and we would not have the stories we now laugh about. We need to keep our heads and our sense of humor in the midst of these challenges. In all seriousness therapy is extremely helpful and needed for all families, never be afraid to reach for support.

Being honest though, have you ever been just a bit jealous of those Hallmark movies? You can't help but love the messages and the perfection of each family at the end. Oh, and you get to cry too. These movies are filled with grace. Secretly, wouldn't you love to have the perfect Hallmark Christmas family photo? Let's be realistic, trying to get everyone ready can be a nightmare!

I guess what we are trying to share with you is to allow and give yourself grace. Don't try to be perfect, be yourself with all the bells, whistles, and flaws. You'll be happier in the long run.

GET READY TO BE HUMBLED

This is not a "how to" book for this reason. Every family, circumstance, experience, and every person involved is different. We know this with even traditional families: what works for one may not work for the other. We're just multiplying the odds. It's like playing with an etch-a-sketch each day. Wouldn't it be great to yell "Do over!"

One of my most humbling moments was when the local newspaper was looking for a family to do an article about morning schedules. How to get the family up and out the door. I let someone talk me into contacting the paper. Sure enough, we were selected to be interviewed and to have a photographer come to take pictures of our "hectic" morning routines. What did I do, I made sure we were "perfect" that morning for when the photographer came. I even directed the conversation during the interview. Who was I trying to impress? The results were disastrous. Do I wish we could have gotten a "do over." Absolutely! I was embarrassed, the pictures were horrible, and of course, in my mind, "everyone" knew about it and read the article! We were not perfect. Our focus should have been on who we were. One determined family trying to get five children to five different places and two parents off to work on time.

You are going to make mistakes. You are going to be emotionally triggered. You are going to do and say the wrong things. You are going to be hated. But then, if you really want to make it work, you will need to put aside being perfect and look for the opportunities to step up, step aside, and step down. Have grace.

If you wish to read more specifically on how to parent with grace, we found "Step Parenting with Grace," by Gayla Grace. Ms. Grace also has a community for Stepparents at SteparentingWithGrace. com. It's always good to have additional resources.

TRUST THE PROCESS...

When working on developing a new trusting relationship, think back to dating. For the majority of us, we all start off slow trusting in relationships. We get to know a person, their likes, their dislikes, favorite foods, hobbies, music, talents, and so forth. As a biological parent, you know most of these attributes; as a bonus parent, you start at the beginning. When we are blending families, we should be doing the same with each child.

Trust takes time. Trust is about your verbal commitments and your actions. Your promises. Keeping your door open. How do you show someone you can be trusted or that you trust them?

If you have watched the movie "Meet the Parents," where Greg Focker feels like an outsider in girlfriend Pam's family, you might have felt you can relate to Greg's plight. No matter what Greg does, he seems to make each situation worse and is constantly being reminded by Pam's father, Jack, that he's watching him. As Jack takes Greg in, he explains the purpose of the Byrnes Family "Circle of Trust" and asks Greg if he wants to be part of the circle. Long story short, Greg decides that he and Pam need to create their new circle of trust, and if her dad wants to be a part of their life, a part of their circle, Jack must be willing to move forward.

● ● ●

My relationship with the children has generally been smooth sailing compared to what I thought it was going to be. I was expecting it to be very challenging, but honestly because my husband set the stage of respect and love for me, the children followed his lead. I can't reiterate enough that the way the parents lead is how the children will follow, good or bad. The harder part has been with the in-laws and exes. It was surprising because the resistance seemed to come much more strongly after my spouse and I were married.

Trust is a two-way street. Just like we need to foster an environment that allows our children to trust us, we need to trust them as well. It's not always the child who may feel left out, maybe it's the bonus parent. Let's use this circle of trust as a metaphor for how we might create our new circle of trust. When there is an existing bond between bio-parents and their children, the new bonus parent naturally will feel left out of the current circle of trust. How do we move forward in creating a new circle? One parent shared her intentional awareness to include **_all_** family members on text messages, social posts, group chats, and video chats.

• • •

Our blended family has been in place for over twenty years. It wasn't until this past year that I think I finally understood what the power of belonging means to a stepchild. We have celebrated Christmas the same way each year since I married their father, with a few exceptions here and there. My stepchildren are older and no longer need to follow a holiday plan for who goes where. As adults, they can choose how they wish to spend the holiday. When the children were younger, they spent Christmas Eve and Christmas morning with us, and then we would take them to their mothers for the rest of Christmas Day.

Once the three older children left to go to their mothers, the remaining four of us would go over to my parent's home for Christmas Day dinner, games, and other family traditions. This year their biological mother was out of town with their sister, and the boys were here locally. When it came time to go over to my parents' home, naturally, I assumed we were all going. Only to hear my stepson say, "I'll just stay here, and you guys can celebrate Christmas with your family." It stopped me in my tracks. I never thought of my family as anything other than "his/ their" family. We talked, and he did come for Christmas dinner with my parents, but it was his first time with this tradition that the rest of us had done for years. When you think you have finally made it over that hill, there's another one yet to climb.

• • •

One of my step nephews said to me, "I always liked going to your house for Christmas because you always made us feel welcome." I didn't appreciate his kind words until we gathered all these perspectives from our respondents. It is important for children to feel like they "belong" to a new family. Accepted. Loved. However, if you ask his young sister, she will say, "I don't like that mean Aunt!" Well, we can't be perfect!

We've spent a lot of focus on being aware of how the children can be embraced in this new world, but we haven't addressed how the adult's blend. While speaking with one of our respondents, she said that growing as a bonus parent was a process. The reality is we entered the "game" late. The ground rules are set, and when we are coming in as the reserve player, we have to find a way to fit in on the team. These rules or traditions are embedded in how the children were first raised with their instilled values and beliefs.

> *"The first key to balancing your busy life and creating a peaceful environment for your blended family to thrive lies in defining your family values - first as a couple, then as a family."*
> ~ KELLYE LAUGHERY

As you grow in the process, these rules and traditions will keep revealing themselves. At these points, it's hard not to be reactive; as a bonus parent, remind yourself to step back and pause. Take a moment to understand the situation and the individuals involved. In most cases, no one is actively trying to exclude you. (Well maybe.) Keep reminding yourself that it's a process and may take years.

Because many families are formed on traditions, as we discussed earlier, we now have an opportunity to create a new sense of belonging for all members with new traditions. Continuing to celebrate traditions is essential, and now is an opportunity to focus on some new ones, especially when you have yours, mine, and ours. These new traditions will be decided by all new family members. How awesome, is this, to have everyone's input on what to do as a family, to create new memories with involvement from all!

Some might be simple, such as every Sunday going on a family bike ride and stopping for ice cream, or a family movie or game night. Or maybe it's an annual trip to a place that you all have decided on, like a Cabin on a Lake, and here you start your new traditions, games, foods, ask and find out what you can do. You meet new people who have nothing to do with anyone's past, and it's a fresh new start. The purpose is for everyone to be on the same level playing field. You get to decide the ground rules and develop your new traditions together.

Sometimes we won't know how valuable these moments we create are until much later. At our daughter's wedding, her mother had this fun emoji story to celebrate all the women who have supported her daughter throughout her lifetime. She included all family and friends in the order these women appeared in her life. I was so happy to have been included, and my emoji of a *"Home and Dinner"* was held up by me as she shared the story. For my part, she said her favorite memories at our home were the meals we sat down for, and the times we talked around the kitchen island eating with her, her brothers, and friends.

You may not think these small traditions matter, but even now, when all the children get together, they all go to the kitchen, start foraging for snacks, make drinks and before you know it, the laughter begins. The kitchen is the place they feel connected with one another.

We think it's fair to say we have read a lot of books and thought we had a good grasp of creating a bonded new family. We also know there were times we decided to wing it. We feel it's safe to say we all thought we had a very well-planned strategy in place. Maybe we need to start to think blended families are more like an etch-a-sketch, and just when you think you have it all figured out how to use the knobs and finally create something decent, someone decides to shake it up! Try again!

One of the sweetest stories shared was with a respondent who is both a bio and bonus parent. She said she learned more from her daughter in creating belonging with all members. Her daughter is divorced but _includes her ex-husband in everything!_ She said it's not easy for her, as he is not her favorite person, but to their son, he is! Her daughter set aside her feelings to ensure everyone still feels included. She said she is amazed at her daughter's perspective, the kindness shown and awareness of her son's feelings over hers.

NEW TRADITIONS AND HOLIDAYS - HONORING OUR PAST WHILE CREATING A NEW FUTURE

STEPPING TOGETHER

Stepping aside from all you've known about holidays and traditions, really honoring what they had in place that the children love and starting from scratch with your new family for some new traditions can be a breath of fresh air.

Making new traditions can be particularly helpful as a new blended family. Keeping traditions that are truly valued by the children while incorporating your own new family activities creates a good feeling.

Plan and lower expectations for the big days, particularly Father's Day and Mother's Day. These are doozies for blended families because there are such high expectations. It had been a particularly rocky day with some highlights and it was 10 p.m. when my bonus son showed up to give me a hug on the special parent day. It touched my heart forever. I hadn't expected him to come over so it was a great experience rather than one of expectation or pressure. Talking through events can help with this as well.

• • •

For our son's military graduation, he only had a couple of hours of free time to spend with family, both biological and stepparents who had traveled to the ceremony. We told him that whatever he wanted to do during that time would be fine with us! He decided to split his time in half, and we all enjoyed our quality time with him.

As your children get older, including them in their own experiences with shared parenting time will help them to feel supported and not caught in the middle. Just remember to keep your expectations with things you can control. For instance, I can control that I will not talk unkindly or be selfish with time. I can't control what anyone else does.

"Becoming a blended family means mixing, mingling, scrambling, and sometimes muddling our way through delicate family issues, complicated relationships, and individual different hurts, and fears. But through it all, we are learning to love like a family."

~TOM FRYDENGER

New activities that may help show value of the new blended family include:

- **Sand art exercises:** Each family member has a different color of sand, then they each pour them into a container to make a combined family design.
- **Cut down a Christmas tree together:** Low engagement is needed for this, and most children think it's fun.
- **Baking and cook in the kitchen:** Food can be particularly special because you can do it during any holiday.
- **Plant a family tree or garden:** Create a garden where everyone can participate and decide on a plant or veggie they like.
- **Holiday pajamas:** The whole family will share in unity, and what a great photo!

- **Run or walk a 5k together:** With all the same "team" name on your new family t-shirts.

The Holidays can be the most stressful times with trying to get all the traditional planning done, and now in a blended family and trying to work around the schedule to meet everyone's needs. Stepping aside from all of your own ways of doing things and instead melding together a new set of past traditional and new special moments can make all the difference during important holidays.

If you are a master color coded chart person, you might just thrive with all the planning, but only 45% of the population's temperament is naturally organized this way, which allows for about 40% of the population to be the direct opposite! We said it before, no wonder we have conflict.

Who gets who and who gets to celebrate when...well let's look at what the Divorce decree states or let's be adults and work out a meaningful schedule.

Which holidays are important to you? Now is not the time to be difficult just to be in control but rather focus on what matters.

- For example, in one situation a husband enjoyed hunting season and his ex-wife's family celebrated Thanksgiving. When they were married, she always went to her family's Thanksgiving as her grandma made the best riced potatoes. So why not keep that the same? Traditions are important for the children to experience.
- For my husband, Memorial Day, 4th of July, and Labor Day weekends were important to him and his family, as they would go up to the lake with his parents to fish and play at the lake.
- Halloween, who ever had, the children at the time or celebrates it more energetically.
- Easter was very important for one particular ex-wife – she would have a big Easter egg hunt for the children and really looked forward to it. I didn't grow up with Easter Egg hunts, I never organized them for my children, and I am glad I

didn't. I never wanted to make a wonderful holiday tradition that she did or grew up with and enjoyed with our children to be viewed as a competition. This is important to understand as a bonus parent, please don't try to take away something that is special just "because." We focused on the baskets, she focused on the Egg Hunt. The best of two worlds.

- I want to share an experience my stepdaughter created for her half-brothers when we were visiting over my youngest son's birthday and Easter. When we arrived at their home, it was our youngest son's birthday. One tradition I would do for all the children is making their birthday cakes. I always thought having a special cake was important. My stepdaughter made sure to have a cake for him. I would like to think that was my influence in celebrating all the children' birthdays. We had a special homemade cake! A few days later was Easter. She planned an Easter Egg hunt for her brothers and even included her father and me. This was the first time they had EVER experienced an Easter Egg hunt. It was so special. To this day, it's an experience they share together and may decide to do with their families.
- Christmas has always been important to my Husband. So, he and his ex-wife worked it out to have Christmas Eve and Christmas morning at our house, then in the morning we would take the children to mom's for the rest of Christmas day. When it came to Easter, we would tell the children they had a special basket delivered. I do remember the children celebrating St. Nick's day in December. Again, nothing I did in my family, but a tradition we made sure to keep going for the children if they were at our house overnight. Keep those traditions.
- My first Christmas as a bonus mother, I remember my husband's ex wife giving us a zip lock bag of cracker crumbs and glitter to have the children sprinkle outside as "reindeer food." I remember first thinking, does "she" think I don't know what to do? Well, she was right, I would not have done this without her guidance and again, it wasn't about who was

in the "right" but what we can do to make the holiday special for the children regardless of where they are. Remember this!

- Oh, where to begin. The first Christmas we spent as a blended family when I was a child, my stepmom bought my sister, brothers, stepsisters, and me matching sweatshirts and hats. All six of us children made a pyramid. We all laughed about the matching outfits and secretly made fun, but it brought us together. We were all teenagers at that point so my stepmom had her hands full. She and my dad are celebrating their 25th wedding anniversary.

"Step Mother: one who does all the things that a biological mom does, yet gets rejected and degraded regardless of how great she is. She loves and cares for another's child with all she has while denying her own happiness. She invests her heart and soul into a child that she did not birth. She sustains mistreatment and unfairness, yet remains steadfast in her battle. She is portrayed as a monster, although she is a saint. She waits and hopes for the day that she will be acknowledged, appreciated, accepted and loved. For she too is a Mother."

~UNKNOWN

- I invited my bonus son to come hunting with me and even just asking him really made him feel welcome and part of my experience.
- We celebrate unique days to make sure there are fun traditions in our family. This might mean we make a big deal out of a sporting event, baptism, or movie release. This way we are celebrating all year round and less focused on the Hallmark holidays.
- Our family makes an attempt to go pick-out a Christmas tree every year, together. We alternate who gets to cut down the tree. Nearly all of our children come every year. This was a new tradition we started. I think it's been a huge success

because their bio parents had never done it with them, it felt new, like our own families.

- We have a family meeting every Sunday night of the school year. Since many of our children are grown and live in different states now, this 30-minute meeting where we open with prayer and then share openly about what's going on in our lives is a tradition for us to stay connected.
- During special traditions that are important to our coparents, we step aside and create a compromise to ensure that, if at all possible, the children get to experience the best of both worlds.
- We regularly take a trip every year to visit extended family. This was so important to me that I actually asked to write it into our divorce agreement so that it wouldn't be a battle every year.
- We have had four weddings in five years (including ours). This has presented many opportunities to interact with "in-laws" and "ex's." Moms can get very territorial and aggressive about their children when the new spouse is around. Unfortunately, it became a bit heated at one of the weddings. My daughter-in-law's relationship with her mom and stepmom has been forever damaged. No matter "why" a marriage ended, the mom has deep love for the children. If you are a stepmom, honor that. Love them oodles and oodles when it is your time. We can either help each other be the best version or worst version of ourselves in front of our children and bonus children. We must learn to deal with situations when difficult things get really tough.
- No matter what, my stepdaughter's mother and I take her to her first day of school. It's great to have a tradition together for the child. She is eight and in second grade. We've been taking her together since she was in pre-kindergarten.

● ● ●

My mom married my dad at age 20 after his wife died. He was 35 and had three children. To this day we are the GREAT 8! Brothers and sisters as one. Our mom is now 88 years old!

REFLECTIONS FROM THOSE WE INTERVIEWED

We want to share the collective feedback from many blended families we surveyed and interviewed. Below are the questions and many responses. Take their advice, experiences, and missteps to help you become more successful with your blended family. It is our way to be your village!

What is the most challenging part of becoming a blended family?

- Putting differences aside for the children. It's hard. But you have to look in the mirror and make the decision to be and do better.
- Understanding that perspectives of parenting may be different than what you would do, but that does not make different ways of parenting wrong.
- Finding common ground. Everyone must be willing to give and take.
- Your co-parents may not want to cooperate with you at all. They may be jealous of you and try to do very harmful things. They may not want your family to succeed. Succeed anyway by taking the higher road.
- An insecure, vengeful or fearful parent can choose to limit their child, to use negativity to build up walls, make the child choose sides while a positive parent can create an

environment of support, open communication, confidence and enough love. Be the second type of co parent.

Please use this space to journal your thoughts or responses:

_____

_____

_____

_____

_____

What is a blessing about being a blended family that more traditional families miss out on?

- There are SO MANY, be willing to look for the blessings and not rips.
- The children knowing their parents work to communicate will make them feel more secure. If we work on communication well, the ties of family are not separated, but hold strong.
- Knowing our children are able to do so much more and enjoy being part of a larger family with lots of grandpas and grandmas, aunts, uncles and cousins.
- Most often the children get the best version of their parents because when custody is shared there is time for each parent to recuperate, clean, stock up; take in needed self-care time.
- It truly takes a village to raise children and with a blended family the village just got bigger and more supportive!

Please use this space to journal your thoughts or responses:

_____

_____

_____

_____

_____

What is one tip I would give to a bonus parent?

- Your role as a parent is not any less difficult or less purposeful.
- There will be days where you feel depleted, that know you could have done better and could have been a better parent. It happens to the best of us.
- You truly care for the child and those feelings are completely normal. Because you feel you could do better and be better, you will try every day.
- Your role is no less important than the role of a biological parent, in fact, it is even more admirable. You made room in your heart and home to love another, you chose to love this child (children).
- Love covers a multitude. Be gracious, with your new family members and yourself.
- Give yourself grace. If you are doing your best, that is enough for the day - even when it doesn't feel like it.
- Ok, that's three, but you need them all to make it work. Put yourself in their shoes.
- Patience and communication between you and your spouse. Lots of grace.
- Be fair, love unconditionally.
- Always be open and understanding. Don't place blame.
- Your relationship with your stepchild is its own unique relationship that needs love, attention, and care. In my situation, I met my bonus son when he was two and really was an all-in bonus mom. Even after his biological father and I divorced, he is a part of my everyday life. He is now in his late twenties and often shares with me that I am a part of

why he is where he is today, and he loves me dearly. Being a bonus mom or dad doesn't need to be a bad thing. In fact, if you treat it like your other relationships with intentionality, it can be a wonderful thing.

- Put yourself in their shoes.
- Be great at compromise!
- Love them as though they were your own.
- Be patient. Listen. Love.
- When big changes happen, such as a divorce, children may often feel awkward, tense, sad, or very unsettled. They may be pulled in many directions and to them it feels like a million directions. They're stressed enough. Be understanding and check in on them often. Do your best to keep the situation neutral. Don't create any new rules that would cause tension for them or the rest of the household if possible. Be understanding of what they are going through. Their world is getting flipped upside down.
- Pray with your spouse daily about parenting your children and back each other up on big parenting decisions.
- Remember to keep it about the children. Divorce can bring out the ugly in the nicest people. Putting the children first and love your new stepchildren with all your heart!
- There is a better chance, everything will fall into place when you put the children first.
- Patience. Listen. Only give advice if asked. Empathy.
- Love covers a multitude. Be gracious...with your new family members and with yourself.
- Stay neutral to the relationship of your spouse and their children.
- A divorce, remarriage, or new relationship, it is not the child's fault. Let the focus and love be on the children.
- Hang in there. It gets very difficult at times but it's well worth it if you see the good things that come of it.

- The "other parent" is not always easy to deal with and you may "not always" agree, but what's important is the child, not your opinions or likes/dislikes of the other parent.
- Don't ever say something negative about the child's biological parent to anyone.
- Have patience; every child is different.
- Take things slow.
- Allow the children to be who they were made to be. Love them no matter what.
- Allow them to love their other parents without guilt.
- Spend time getting to know your stepchildren and what they need. Provide support to them without taking over the role their biological parent provides. At the same time, you may very well be able to fill in the role the biological parent has chosen not to provide.
- Get involved in the rearing of all children.
- Try your best to treasure your bonus children "as much as" your bio children. I've never been a stepparent, only a step/bonus child, so I'm not sure of all the ins and outs of that role.
- Love them well. Don't try to change them (especially if they are older).
- Remember they are dealing with baggage from their parent's past relationships.
- As a biological parent, I know my children, how they've been raised, and where they are at emotionally. With bonus children, you don't always have a full understanding of where they've come from and who they are. Be patient as you grow this relationship.

Please use this space to journal your thoughts or responses:

_____

_____

_____

_____

_____

What is one tip that you would give a biological parent?

- Communication is so important. Most common issues stem from miscommunication or a misunderstanding, especially when co-parenting. Have patience, back one another up at all times and always respect the other parent(s).
- Co-parenting is difficult, at first, because you have to put aside your pride and be open to other ideas and suggestions. You have to build and maintain another relationship, keep in contact with a former partner, be understanding, forgiving, and respectful. Try to put your needs last. Then, it becomes the most natural and easiest relationship to maintain because you all have the same desire; to raise well-mannered and loved children. It is easier to love than to hate. It feels much more rewarding to encourage and build one another up than tear each other down.
- Holding on to grudges, being selfish and hateful makes a person ugly.

Co-parenting is not a competition. It's a collaboration of two homes working together with the best interest of the child at heart. Work for your children, not against them."

~UNKNOWN

- My husband's ex once sent an elf on a shelf home with our daughter for us to do it at our house without any conversation about doing it before. Don't do that kind of stuff, respect that we have our own full plate of things to do and don't add on arbitrarily without asking first.

- Once you realize how truly easy and incredible it is to be a big extended family rather than a split household, you can encourage other families to do the same, and watch the love grow.
- Co-parenting may not seem easy from the outside looking in, but from the inside, it _is_.
- The stepparent doesn't have to, and isn't likely trying to, replace you. See the blessing in another person loving and caring for your child/ren. This is also hugely helpful and important for the child/ren.
- Cooperation and communication are key. Don't be threatened, it's best for all to work together.
- Understand that the love you feel for your child may not be exactly the same feelings that the bonus parent is going to feel. However, it does not mean the bonus parent doesn't love your child.
- Remember to love. Be patient and kind. Navigating these new waters is challenging for everyone involved.
- Never blame or put down others.
- Keep lines of communication open.
- Be the foundation the child needs. If the child does not get along with the spouse you now have, don't let that get in the way of you having a relationship with your child. I'm not saying you have to pick and choose but try to ensure your spouse takes the high road and doesn't get upset that you want to have one on one time with your child.
- We got this if you can be a team player.
- Don't play sides. Be a parent and welcome the bonus parent to be treated as a parent as well.
- You may have to change your parenting style a bit to make it fit in your new family.
- Make sure your children still know they're a priority. Sometimes the honeymoon phase of a new marriage can make us feel left out, not important

- For our biological children, it's important to allow the children to move into the new blended family at their own pace. Some children accept the scenario right away and others need to ease their hearts and minds into it. We see many families get this critical step wrong by pushing their children into accepting "my new husband." It all boils down to each parent earning their trust.
- Focus on the happiness of your child.
- I love your child too.
- Treat everyone equally, especially the children.
- Your family just got bigger. Not smaller.
- We encourage you to really talk through parenting and establish who will have the final say with the children before you get married.
- Do everything you can to make space for and check in with your kiddo's feelings. They may need time with just you even if you're falling in love with a new partner and don't realize it.
- Don't play favorites. It hurts. Try to be open minded and always be kind. Understand that the love you feel for your child may not be exactly the same feelings that the bonus parent is going to feel. However, it does not mean the bonus parent doesn't love your child.

"Every parent has the ability to free their child from a loyalty bind by saying, "It's okay to like or love your stepparent. I want you to have a wonderful relationship with them. There's enough love to go around."
~ U N K N O W N

Please use this space to journal your thoughts or responses:

_____

_____

_____

_____

_____

What is the role of a bonus parent and what does it really mean to you?

- It means that you will always have another co-parent for the rest of your life. Pause and take that in for a couple minutes.
- You are choosing to submit a lot of your plans, what you will or won't have control over many things based on becoming part of a stepfamily.
- There is a certain beauty in letting go of expectations and control of everything. But there may also be a constant pull, or additional check-ins that need to happen, as you plan for activities, holidays, and special events.
- It is a common misconception that you, as the bonus parent, are going to come in and change things, make them "better," stand-up for your partner in a new way. Some of these happen naturally but for most some stepparents they come to the harsh reality that they don't have a voice, or call, as it relates to much of the schedule, expenses, and overall interactions change.
- Make sure your expectation is on target with what you will and won't have control of. For instance, are you and your new spouse able to move if needed? Are you able to travel frequently or does the schedule dictate remaining close to home? Are you marrying into a long term payment commitment that has been ordered by the court that will now become a part of your family budget every year.
- Time - take the time to get to know who has to get to know each other. This is really paramount with the stepfamily dynamic. I will never forget the time that my stepchild invited me to a major event. I truly felt surprised and overjoyed. I had done a good job of setting my expectations

low after many previous times of things just not happening how I thought they would. What I realized is that all of that time, loving them well (not perfectly), being patient, showing love and kindness over them was actually sowing a relationship that was a treasure.

> "They call it a 'stepfamily' because together
> we took a step in the right direction."
>
> ~ UNKNOWN

- In a way, the blended family dynamic is like a slow-moving train. It takes a long time to really get to a destination and you have very little control over many dynamics. Rest on the observation deck, enjoy the view, and when they need you to help show the way, are some of the keys to blending parenting gracefully.

- It's important to understand that while being fair if you have multiple types of children (adopted, biological, bonus), each relationship is indeed unique and evolves at its own pace. Rushing these relationships and trying to force feelings is the quickest way to have them take even longer. It can be challenging to pace yourself as it relates to your new relationships with your spouse's family but there is wisdom in having a paced rhythm of consistency and taking your bonus child's lead.

- One stepchild we spoke with shared what their bonus parent could have done differently when they first met them and started interacting more frequently. The stepchild actually said it was ok to ask about their interests, invite them places and be a bit more engaged with the relationship. There can be a tendency for the stepparent to either be very withdrawn or very involved at first, but a nice balance seems to be more appropriate. If in doubt, and your bonus children are age appropriate, just ask. Children are very honest and will tell you how they feel about how you're doing and what you can do differently.

- As there is a collection of perspectives on how to address a stepparent (we've used bonus parent/child interchangeably in this book), allow all those involved to come up with a term that is acceptable and comfortable. Maybe we address with first names, a nickname, or maybe the relationship allows for individuals to use "Mom or Dad." Regardless, give this time.
- When our children are born and given to us, we automatically have earned being called "mother or father." When a divorce happens, typically, these titles remain. If anything, they may be expanded when parents remarry or are in other relationships. Having the opportunity to fulfill both roles, we must sometimes be respectful of the relationship we have. As a mother and recognizing that some of our children are spending half of their lives with their biological mom and a new person whom they call "mom" it is understandable how this small word can break a heart. We think titles don't matter, but they do to some, and we need to understand how titles can make others feel. Please take a moment to ask and respect our roles and never force. If it's meant to be it will happen naturally and will have more meaning in the end.
- Don't be discouraged if the process takes longer than you would like. Every relationship has its own pace with its own twists and turns.

"If you're struggling with your role, be kind to yourself and remember that step parenting is one of the hardest things you'll ever do. Not because of any flaw of yours, but because that's the nature of the role."

~JENNA KORI

Please use this space to journal your thoughts or responses:

_____

_____

_____

_____

_____

How should I interact on social media as it relates to my blended family?

- Being conscious and aware of social media impacts is very important. Your partner's ex may not wish to see any of your posts or may choose to. I recommend always posting as if they can see it. How would you feel and how would your bonus children feel?
- Never post anything that would cause pain.
- Think about all postings from the child's perspective.

Please use this space to journal your thoughts or responses:

_____

_____

_____

_____

_____

What is a blessing about being a blended family?

- Building a friendship with someone you otherwise normally would not have in order to help your stepchildren grow and become healthy adults. From all perspectives, overcoming the challenges together are what make it so rewarding.
- The opportunity to positively impact the lives of other/more children.

- Learning to be gracious in turmoil and how to navigate the stresses of not just your spouse but their ex.
- In my case, now divorced and still having a relationship with that "step" and being part of his married family!
- You gain a different perspective, and it teaches you to always consider others feelings and not take them for granted
- The combining of different households, traditions, and personalities.
- One of the biggest joys has been showing my oldest daughters the role a father should be playing in their lives. My ex-wife and I added two of our own biological children to her existing family.
- How you learn to work through challenges and see completely different viewpoints. Creating new family traditions.
- The combining of different households, traditions, and personalities.
- The opportunity to positively impact the lives of other/more children.
- Unconditional love reaches beyond typical traditional direct family.
- You get more challenges to navigate at times but also a broader perspective.
- Making new family traditions.
- More people to love and to love on you.
- I didn't have to go through the birth of having him and still get to love him well.
- The opportunity to have bonus parents and siblings.
- Having a larger family is great. Constantly learning more about yourself as you are challenged with new and different situations.
- The opportunity to help with a different perspective of the birth parent
- Redemption. Every hope and dream we prayed for is being fulfilled through our family with the understanding that

Christ is the center. Hopefully our children will see stability can exist if we keep Christ the center of our home.

- You learn that love is beyond blood relation.
- The age span offers the chance to learn about different generations. My oldest half-sister is 10 years older, and my youngest brother is 10 years younger. 8 siblings. Huge family. 55 people.
- Multiple children of the same age, without the sibling rivalry. It's like a group of friends!
- The child gets double the love!
- The child gets to experience different homes, family interactions and parenting styles.
- Having additional resources from both families, each bonus parent has their own specialty and is a knowledge expert in their own way and has had previous life experience. I have double the assistance if I ever need it.
- So many people are there for you and support the family
- Being a part of a larger extended family.
- Help heal the brokenness in the stepchildren's hearts.

● ● ●

I am thankful for the opportunity to strengthen each of who they are through the unity that comes from being a blended family. The rewards of those moments when we're in sync are some of my favorite moments ever and I am gratefully surprised to see the moments of growth, connection and beauty through-out our blended lives.

Please use this space to journal your thoughts or responses:

_____

_____

_____

_____

_____

What has been the most challenging part of being a blended family?

- Inconsistency between households which doesn't allow for a grip on things like household expectations, accountability, discipline, schedules, routines and more.
- Understanding your place and when to step in or give advice. Specifically, when to discipline or when you have different views on the consequences to be imposed.
- The biggest issue I have experienced is getting the stepchildren to understand that I love them just like I love their siblings.
- Keeping insecurities at bay because you're the new person to the family (and knowing that when I was a child, I didn't accept the new family right away)
- You really must earn trust and respect. It's not a natural given like your natural born family. Sometimes there are obstacles to earning that on both sides.
- Making the family feel all equal when one member visits a separate family.
- How important inclusion and communication is and that it's ok to feel defeated some days. I'm a stepchild and a stepparent so I can say that it's important from both sides.
- Forgiving parents for the breakdown of your family and learning to accept the new family members.
- Learning to be gracious in turmoil and how to navigate the stresses of not just your spouse but their ex. Building a friendship with someone you otherwise normally wouldn't to help you stepchildren grow and become healthy adults. From all perspectives, overcoming the challenges together are what make it so rewarding.
- Favoritism. Disciplining. Money. Unfairness.
- Learning about new people and their emotions in a family environment.
- Keeping the peace.

- Agreeing on ways to discipline our children.
- Stepping back or out of the decisions at times.
- Sharing time, being away from my son when he goes with his father.
- Making sure my son is treated the same as my daughter by my new in-laws.
- Earning the trust of our bonus children. They hold their hearts close to themselves early on. It's like peeling an onion and allowing memories to slowly grow and become. There is no such thing as an instant family. Step parents need to offer extra grace, patience, and sacrifice to earn that trust. Time. Lots of time. Children don't want to be pressured to accept this new normal.
- Realizing that our separate children may not be friends.
- Talk to other families and get perspective. Ask your children how they think it's going. Be willing to say you messed up when you did, because no book can prepare you for this daily knuckle biter.
- Parenting styles that were different. We got married when 4 out of 5 were grown. So patterns of "we just do it that way" were set in stone already.
- Having to share the child with a whole other family. Holidays can get so difficult.
- Children don't want to lose their parents to a new girlfriend or boyfriend. They also don't want to get attached to someone who may leave in a month to a year. What we did was not involve the children in our relationship until after a year. And only after knowing we were going to stay together. During this time be careful to move out of the way of parenting of the bio parent. The children don't trust you yet and a simple I agree with your mom goes a long way to build that trust.
- Sharing holidays with a former spouse.

Please use this space to journal your thoughts or responses:

_____

_____

_____

_____

_____

• • •

When I was young I did not feel like I totally belonged in either household.

- Parenting and blending with teenagers. You are each used to how "your" child behaves. Ex: one parent handles attitudes better because they dealt with that from early on with that bio child but step parent struggles. Other child whines and bio parent handles since that's their normal, stepparent's struggles.
- Understanding Fairness, whomever coined the phrase "Life is not fair" must have been talking about blended families. Not going to lie, but fairness can be a difficult concept for our families. How do you not play "favorites' '? We have an ongoing joke in our family about who is the "favorite" today … Everyone is the favorite at some point, but we all know there is a bit of truth and harsh reality we must face. We have even heard the siblings call one of them the "Golden Child." Which led to a great Christmas White Elephant gift of a "black sheep" hat that year. It's all-in fun, but again we can't dismiss there are real feelings behind those thoughts and actions. There is always a bit of truth behind all sarcasm.

**Other suggestions you may have on how
to succeed as a blended family?**

- The importance of showing your children that you are all on one team
- Find a way to keep the peace with the other parent if blended due to divorce or separation. Sometimes you may have to close your mouth and just keep your thoughts to yourself. You don't always have to be right or prove a point. The only people who lose when you fight are the children. Be humble. And pray more than you ever have before. Pray for your new children, your own children, your spouse, the ex and all of the family members involved.
- I think it's important to still allow each child to be their own person. I also think it's vitally important for the adult couple in the household to take time together, talk about co-parenting the children and working together with the exes/other parents involved. We have been intentional about having one-on-one and two adults-on-one time with our combined children and I think that has also been helpful, so the children don't feel they're always "fighting" for attention.
- Show patience and kindness, set aside time to do "family" game night if some sort of activity as a family to make them feel welcome.
- Keep your finger on the pulse
- Communication between all children and parents is necessary. There may be many differences in how the biological parent has raised their child with the ideas that the step-parent brings to the relationship. This is where teamwork is required.

• • •

My biological mother passed away while leaving three little girls aged 9, 7, 3. God blessed our family with a very loving stepmother who shaped and changed our lives for HIS very best. Forever grateful.

- Love, love, love

- Always think of the family unit first. I love my brother's whole family no matter if they're my brothers full children or step children
- Ask yourself if you are being your best self in the situation or conflict. Challenge yourself if you are acting territorial, controlling or irrationally to get back on the path that's best for your child and co-parent.
- Counseling or a course such as Divorce Care after marriage to heal the wounds from the previous marriage.
- When everyone gets along, the children thrive.
- Be humble. And pray more than you ever have before. Pray for your new children, your own children, your spouse, the ex and all of the family members involved.
- You really have to earn trust and respect. It's not a natural given like your natural born family. Sometimes there are obstacles to earning that on both sides.
- Spend time with a blended family who has been doing it well longer than you. This will provide instruction but also support and help when you need it.
- Show patience and kindness, set aside time to do "family" game night or some sort of activity as a family to make them feel welcome.
- You are entering a slow cooker, not forcing water to a boil. It takes time to feel like you are a family. Blending is a slow process. Enjoy each day and take it as it comes!
- Do things together! It may be awkward at first, but it'll bring you closer together
- Forgiveness + Mercy + Grace = Peace
- Keep Christ as center. Find a mentor couple.
- Know your resources and research/study blended family dynamics before getting married.
- Acknowledge the other bio parent with your bio children and encourage them to remain connected to them. This gives the child peace of mind that you are not trying to replace them. Allow them to love at their own pace.

- As spouses, daily communication about the day and what's coming the next day/week to ensure your marriage and understanding of all the moving pieces of the family are clear and prioritized.
- Try your best to "get along". No matter how hard. Sometimes it may seem impossible but remember you're in it for the child!
- Give lots and lots of grace, roll with it and have as much fun as possible.
- Respect boundaries.
- Meals around a table are a wonderful thing for us.
- Listen to the children.
- Stepparents being a very active member and having patience for step-children because every child is different from the others. Open communication is a must.
- Don't fight in front of the child.
- Look for the good in each other. Don't have titles such as half or step. Just brother and sister no matter who the parents are.
- Don't play favorites.
- Work out the differences between both sides of a blended family. Divorce happens for many reasons, but if the biological parents have a bad relationship it truly affects the child. Being mature adults and doing what is best for the child should be first, put your differences aside and be on one team.
- Laugh.
- You know you have made an impact when the children want you around and ask you to do things for them or with them. Don't force your way into a parent roll. Just be an adult.
- Don't bring children into grown up things. Work together with all parents even if you don't like each other.
- Try to focus on inclusion and unconditional love. Do not divide. Unite. We need all the help we can get on this journey.

- Pray through the challenges and laugh over the mishaps. Being a parent is challenging all on its own. Throw in a blended family and that's an entire other level of complicated.
- Count your blessings daily.
- Talk a lot. Create emotionally safe ways to check in and communicate.
- It is a different journey with everyone involved since we all come from different backgrounds so will have to be different for each one! Respect, time and compassion mean everything. Some people are there for a long time, others for a short time and others for life! Savor the memories of them.
- As a parent of an adult if you did the work as they grew up the relationship as friends develop after they are grown. This is a huge blessing to know that they trust and appreciate all the training for life.
- Love each different in your own way.

_____

_____

_____

_____

_____

_____

_____

_____

_____

_____

BLENDED FAMILY RESOURCES

Quotes and references peppered through-out this book.

Your network of blended families in church and community.

Bible - Proverbs, 1 Corinthians 13:4-8, Romans 12:10, Ephesians 5:22-33, Ecclesiastes 4:9-12, Genesis 2:18-24, Song of Songs 8:6-7, Colossians 3:14-17, Ephesians 4:2-3.

Apps

AppClose : An app for communication.

Our Family Wizard App: tracks communication, financial requests, important documents, and contact info.

Cozi App: Shared family calendars make co-parenting simpler by giving both parents access to the kids' schedules whenever they need it.

Parenting Apart App: In addition to tracking schedules, apps can be a helpful way to get answers to common co-parenting questions.

2Houses App: Successful co-parenting across two different households requires a lot of communication.

Talking Parents App: shared calendar, store and share files, unalterable records, real-time notifications, expense tracking, and accountable calling.

Co Parently App: Features a custody calendar, messaging, and expense tracking.

Websites

https://relationshipswa.org.au/resources/tip-sheets/parenting-tip-sheets-(1)

https://www.helpguide.org/articles/parenting-family/step-parenting-blended-families.htm

https://www.stepfamilies.info

https://childrenhealth.org

https://bonusfamilies.com/

Trust

https://www.allprodad.com/trust-activities-for-children/

https://helpyourteennow.com/10-team-building-activities-to-do-with-your-family/

https://www.healthline.com/health/parenting/trust-exercises-for-children

Family Activities

https://www.signupgenius.com/home/team-building-activities-teens-families-couples.cfm

Books for Kids

My Parents Are Divorced Too: A Book for Kids by Kids, by Melanie Ford, Steven Ford, Annie Ford, and Jann Blackstone-Ford

Divorce Is Not the End of the World: Zoe's and Evan's Coping Guide for Kids, by Zoe Stern an Even Stern

Dinosaurs Divorce (Dino Tales: Life Guides for Families), by Laurie Krasny Brown

Mom's House, Dad's House for Kids: Feeling at Home in One Home or Two, by Isolina Ricci PhD

Books for Parents

Wisdom On Step-Parenting: How to Succeed Where Others Fail, by Diana Weiss-Wisdom Ph.D.

The Single Girl's Guide to Marrying a Man, His Children, and His Ex-Wife: Becoming a Stepmother with Humor and Grace, by Sally Bjornsen

The Smart Stepfamily: Seven Steps to a Healthy Family, by Ron L. Deal

Step-monster: A New Look at Why Real Stepmothers Think, Feel, and Act the Way We Do, by Wednesday Martin, Ph.D

The Stepmom's Club: How to Be a Stepmom without Losing Your Money, Your Mind, and Your Marriage, by Kendall Rose

Building LOVE together in Blended Families; The 5 Love Languages and Becoming Stepfamily Smart, by Gary Chapman, Ph.D. and Ron L. Deal, MMFT

Step Parenting: 50 One-minute Dos & Don'ts for Stepdads & Stepmoms, by Randall Hicks

Love Languages for Children and Teenagers - Book by Gary Chapman

Healthy Boundaries & Necessary endings - Books by Henry Cloud

The Power of a Praying Parent (Adult Children Version as well) - Book by Stormie Omartian

Co-parenting through Separation and Divorce: Putting your Children First, by Dr. Jann Blackstone

Ex-Etiquette for Holidays and other Family Celebrations, by Dr. Jann Blackstone and Sharyl Jupe

REFERENCES

Blackstone, D. J. (2022, Oct 16). *This wedding breaks 'normal' protocol.* Retrieved from Democratherald.com: https://democratherald. com/ap/lifestyles/wedding-breaks-normal-protocol/article_ 8fef406f-335c-584a-8e01-8185149b6554.html

LIfe.Church. (2022, 4 11). *www.bible.com/bible/111/1CO.13.4-8. NIV.* Retrieved from www.bible.com: https://www.bible.com/ bible/111/1CO.13.4-8.NIV

McLeod, D. S. (2007, 2020, Dec 29). *Simply Psychology.* Retrieved from Simplypsychology.org: https://www.simplypsychology.org

NCTI. (2022, May 22). *NCTI a Resource for Sucess.* Retrieved from https://www.ncti.org/: https://www.ncti.org

Paine, H. (2020, 10 27). *www.news.com.au/lifestyle/home/interiors/ how-to-fold-towels-photo-sparks-online-debate/.* Retrieved from News.com: https://www.news.com.au/lifestyle/home/interiors/ how-to-fold-towels-photo-sparks-online-debate/news-story/9d 2cc00d49026ef6714688936661782d

Pope, S. (2018, November 30). *3 Reasons Why so Many Second and Third Marriages Fail* . Retrieved from Marriage.com : 3 Reasons Why so Many Second and Third Marriages Fail | Marriage.com

Rowling, J. (2022, 6). *www.goodreads.com/quotes/1085520-to- have-been-loved-so-deeply-even-though-the-person.* Retrieved from www.goodreads.com: https://www.goodreads.com/quotes/1085520-to-have-been-loved-so-deeply-even-though-the-person

Rowling, J. (2022, 6). *www.goodreads.com/quotes/7070395-you-are-protected-in-short-by-your-ability-to-love.* Retrieved from Good Reads: https://www.goodreads.com/quotes/7070395-you-are-protected-in-short-by-your-ability-to-love

Smith, N. (2022, Aug). *www.survivedivorce.com/second-marriage-divorce.* Retrieved from Survive Divorce: www.survivedivorce.com/second-marriage-divorce

Unknown. (2022). *htttps://www.lizstoryplanet.com/moral-stories-kids-kindness/a-hole-in-the-fence/.* Retrieved from https://www.lizstoryplanet.com: https://www.lizstoryplanet.com/moral-stories-kids-kindness/a-hole-in-the-fence/

Unknown. (2022). *www.lizstoryplanet.com/moral-stories-kids-kindness/a-hole-in-the-fence.* Retrieved from lizstoryplanet.com: https://www.lizstoryplanet.com/moral-stories-kids-kindness/a-hole-in-the-fence/

Welch, S. (2006, September). *https://www.oprah.com/spirit/suzy-welchs-rule-of-10-10-10-decision-making-guide/all.* Retrieved from Oprah.com: https://www.oprah.com/spirit/suzy-welchs-rule-of-10-10-10-decision-making-guide/all

www.ingramcontent.com/pod-product-compliance
Lightning Source LLC
Chambersburg PA
CBHW020409130626
46549CB00006B/2496